COUNTRY STUDIES

FRANCE

Celia Tidmarsh

Series Editor: John Hopkin

Heinemann Educational Publishers
Halley Court, Jordan Hill, Oxford, OX2 8EJ
A division of Reed Educational &
Professional Publishing Ltd
Heinemann is a registered trademark of Reed
Educational & Professional Publishing Ltd

OXFORD MELBOURNE AUCKLAND
JOHANNESBURG BLANTYRE GABORONE
IBADAN PORTSMOUTH NH (USA)
CHICAGO

First published 1999

ISBN 0 431 01419 1 (Hardback)
    0 431 01420 5 (Paperback)

Tidmarsh, Celia
  France – (Country studies)   20086199
  1. France – Social conditions – 20th century
      – Juvenile literature
  2. France – History – 1945 – Juvenile literature
  3. France – Description and travel – Juvenile
      literature
  I. Title
  944'.0839

03 02 01 00
10 9 8 7 6 5 4 3 2 1

Typeset and illustrated by Hardlines, Charlbury,
Oxford OX7 3PS

Original illustrations © Heinemann Educational
Publishers 1999

Originated by Ambassador Litho
Printed and bound in Spain by Edelvives

Acknowledgements
The publishers would like to thank the following for
permission to reproduce copyright material.

Maps and extracts
p.4 B R Ansell, Landscapes of Brittany / Sunflower
Books, London; **p.4 B** Lonely Planet Guide to France /
Lonely Planet Publications, London; **p.4 B** A Eperon, Lot
(Quercy) / Pan, London; **p.9 C** Eurobarometer 44, Spring
1996, DG X / European Commission, Brussels, Belgium;
p.12 B Collins-Longman Resource Atlas: France /
HarperCollins, London; **p.15 C** Tourist Map 240 /
Michelin Travel Publications; **p.26** Lonely Planet Guide
to France / Lonely Planet Publications, London; **p.26 G**
N Minshull, The New Europe: into the 1990s / Hodder &
Stoughton Educational, London; **p.27 D** Portrait of the
Regions, Volume 1, Eurostat / European Commission,
Luxembourg; **p.28 A** France - a country profile / The
Economist Intelligence Unit, London; **p.29 D** Financial
Times, London; **p.30 A** Montreuil- a European place
study / The Geographical Association, Sheffield; **p.30 B**
Montreuil Tourist Map / Michelin Travel Publications;
p.32 A, C Understanding Global Issues / European
Schoolbooks Limited, Cheltenham; **p.32 C** France in
Figures, 1998 / INSEE, Paris, France; **p.34 B** Portrait of
the Regions, Volume 1, Eurostat / European Commission,
Luxembourg; **p.36 C** Andrew Jack / Financial Times,
London; **p.40 A** France - a country profile / The
Economist Intelligence Unit, London; **p.40 B**, C Collins-
Longman Resource Atlas: France / HarperCollins,
London; **p.42 B** France - a country profile / The
Economist Intelligence Unit, London; **p.44 A** INSEE,
Paris, France; **p.44 B**, **p.46 A** Geography 1991 / The
Geographical Association, Sheffield; **p.46 C** John Ridding
/ Financial Times, London; **p.46 C** Dominique Baudis,
Welcome to Toulouse / Mairie, Toulouse, France; **p.49 C**
Brochure / Rural France Direct, Fordingbridge; **p.51 D**
George Graham / Financial Times, London; **p.52 A** Nice
Tourist Map 245 / Michelin Travel Publications; **p.55 B**
Financial Times, London.

Photographs
Cover photos: Lavender field and farmhouse, Tony Stone
Images; Young people in Paris, Corbis UK
p.5 C Michael Busselle; **p.5 D** Michael Busselle; **p.6 B**
John Heseltine; **p.7 C** Eye Ubiquitous; **p.8 A** AKG;
p.10 A SPL/Geospace; **p.11 B** John Heseltine; **p.11 C**
Michael Busselle; **p.14 A** John Heseltine; **p.14 B** Michael
Busselle; **p.16 B** NHPA/ Eric Soder; **p.17 C** SPL/Dr. Gene
Feldman; **p.19 D** Corbis/Owen Franken; **p.21 D** Frank
Spooner Pictures/Gamma; **p.23 C** Frank Spooner
Pictures/Gamma Press; **p.25 B** The Stock Market; **p.25 C**
Corbis/Paul Almasy; **p.25 D** Sophie Champagnon; **p.25
E** Hutchison Library/Bernard Regent; **p.26 B** SPL/M-SAT
Ltd; **p.28 B** Hutchison Library/Bernard Regent; **p.29 C**
Camera Press/Imapress; **p.31 C** Photo Air; **p.36 B** Rex
Features; **p.36 C** Frank Spooner Pictures/Gamma Press;
p.38 A Hutchison Library/Alan Hutchison; **p.41 D**
Corbis/Marc Garanger; **p.43 C** Courtesy of Elf –
Atochem; **p.43 D** Rex Features/Sipa Press; **p.45 D**
Hutchison Library/Leslie Woodhead; **p.47 D** Robert
Harding Picture Library/Explorer; **p.49 B** Frank Spooner
Pictures/Gamma Press; **p.50 B** Robert Harding Picture
Library/David Hughes; **p.53 C** Rex Features/Sipa Press;
p.53 D Hutchison Library/Christine Pemberton; **p.59 C**
Corbis/Dave G. Houser.

The publishers have made every effort to trace the
copyright holders, but if they have inadvertently
overlooked any, they will be pleased to make the
necessary arrangements at the first opportunity.

For more information about Heinemann Library books,
or to order, please phone 01865 888055, or send a fax to
01865 314091. You can visit our website at
www.heinemann.co.uk

Contents

1 INTRODUCING FRANCE

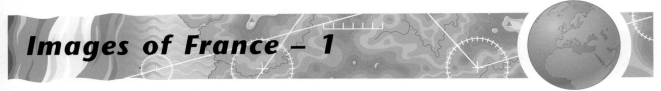

Images of France – 1

▶ What do we know about the landscapes of France?

France is the largest country in Europe and is roughly the shape of a hexagon (map **A**). It has a great variety of physical landscapes, climate, types of settlement and ways of life (figure **B**).

The scenery found here includes flat, rolling plains (photo **C**) and high, rugged mountains (photo **D**). There are large river systems, lakes, salt marshes and different types of coast.

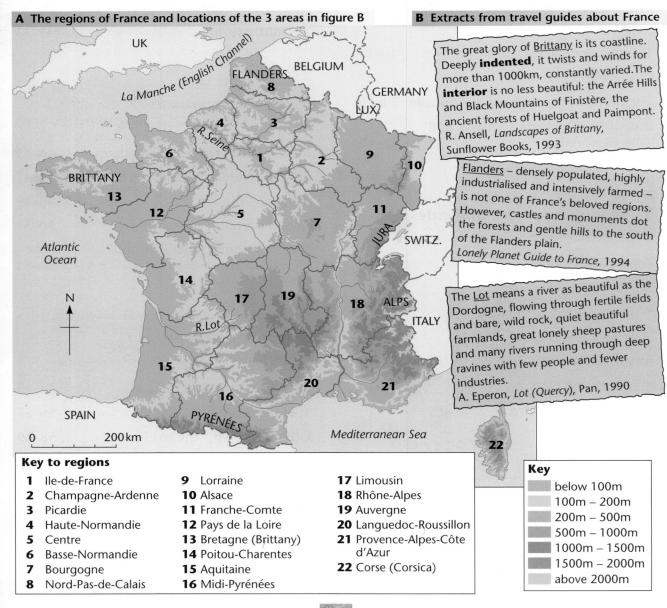

A The regions of France and locations of the 3 areas in figure B

B Extracts from travel guides about France

> The great glory of Brittany is its coastline. Deeply **indented**, it twists and winds for more than 1000km, constantly varied. The **interior** is no less beautiful: the Arrée Hills and Black Mountains of Finistère, the ancient forests of Huelgoat and Paimpont.
> R. Ansell, *Landscapes of Brittany*, Sunflower Books, 1993

> Flanders – densely populated, highly industrialised and intensively farmed – is not one of France's beloved regions. However, castles and monuments dot the forests and gentle hills to the south of the Flanders plain.
> *Lonely Planet Guide to France*, 1994

> The Lot means a river as beautiful as the Dordogne, flowing through fertile fields and bare, wild rock, quiet beautiful farmlands, great lonely sheep pastures and many rivers running through deep ravines with few people and fewer industries.
> A. Eperon, *Lot (Quercy)*, Pan, 1990

Key to regions

1 Ile-de-France	**9** Lorraine	**17** Limousin
2 Champagne-Ardenne	**10** Alsace	**18** Rhône-Alpes
3 Picardie	**11** Franche-Comte	**19** Auvergne
4 Haute-Normandie	**12** Pays de la Loire	**20** Languedoc-Roussillon
5 Centre	**13** Bretagne (Brittany)	**21** Provence-Alpes-Côte d'Azur
6 Basse-Normandie	**14** Poitou-Charentes	**22** Corse (Corsica)
7 Bourgogne	**15** Aquitaine	
8 Nord-Pas-de-Calais	**16** Midi-Pyrénées	

Key

	below 100m
	100m – 200m
	200m – 500m
	500m – 1000m
	1000m – 1500m
	1500m – 2000m
	above 2000m

C Landscape in northern France showing forests and rolling plains

D A variety of landscape features in the Pyrénées

France is bordered by sea – La Manche (English Channel) to the north and west, the Atlantic Ocean to the west and the Mediterranean Sea to the south – and by five other countries to the east and one to the south. Between France and most of these other countries there are natural frontiers of mountains – the Alps and the Jura to the east and the Pyrénées to the south. It is only to the north-east that the frontier between France and the neighbouring countries is flat, low-lying land. The large island of Corsica is part of France and is roughly 180km south-east off the southern coast of France.

FACT FILE

The physical geography of Corsica

Corsica is an island of about 8700sq.km in the Mediterranean Sea. It has a very varied landscape. The inland area is mainly granite mountains, making up about two-thirds of the island. Within them there are about 20 peaks reaching over 2000m. The highest of these peaks is Monte Cinto which is 2706m. The high peaks have snow on them for much of the year. There are also more gentle hills and there is even a desert area, called the Désert des Agriates, to the north of the island. There are about 1000km of coastline with a mixture of high cliffs, low-lying marshland and sandy beaches.

About one-fifth of Corsica is forested, mainly with laricio pine which can live for 600 years and reach a height of 60m. There are also cork oaks and chestnut trees which were once an important source of food on the island. Much of the rest of the island is covered with **maquis** vegetation, which includes undergrowth of lavender, myrtle, rosemary, laurel and thyme. This can become a fire risk in the long dry summer season. Most of the island has a Mediterranean climate with hot, dry summers and mild winters. There is about 900mm of precipitation a year and most of this falls from November to April. For the rest of the year water is likely to be in short supply. Above 1200m there is an alpine climate with cool summers and very cold winters.

Images of France – 2

▶ What do we know about the culture of France?

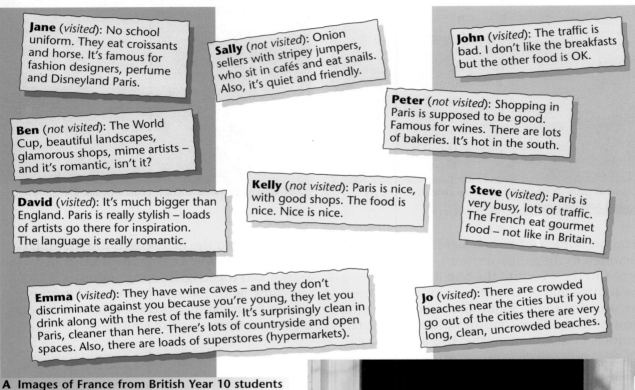

Jane (*visited*): No school uniform. They eat croissants and horse. It's famous for fashion designers, perfume and Disneyland Paris.

Sally (*not visited*): Onion sellers with stripey jumpers, who sit in cafés and eat snails. Also, it's quiet and friendly.

John (*visited*): The traffic is bad. I don't like the breakfasts but the other food is OK.

Ben (*not visited*): The World Cup, beautiful landscapes, glamorous shops, mime artists – and it's romantic, isn't it?

Peter (*not visited*): Shopping in Paris is supposed to be good. Famous for wines. There are lots of bakeries. It's hot in the south.

David (*visited*): It's much bigger than England. Paris is really stylish – loads of artists go there for inspiration. The language is really romantic.

Kelly (*not visited*): Paris is nice, with good shops. The food is nice. Nice is nice.

Steve (*visited*): Paris is very busy, lots of traffic. The French eat gourmet food – not like in Britain.

Emma (*visited*): They have wine caves – and they don't discriminate against you because you're young, they let you drink along with the rest of the family. It's surprisingly clean in Paris, cleaner than here. There's lots of countryside and open spaces. Also, there are loads of superstores (hypermarkets).

Jo (*visited*): There are crowded beaches near the cities but if you go out of the cities there are very long, clean, uncrowded beaches.

A Images of France from British Year 10 students

France is the nearest neighbouring country to the UK. Being neighbours means that people in both countries hear news and form opinions about each other (figure **A**).

From some places on the south coast of England it is possible to see the northern coast of France. Being so close means that, from some parts of England, it is easy to visit even just for a day. The opening of the Channel Tunnel has meant that the journey time to France has become even shorter for people living in the south-east of England.

B Paris fashion houses are famous throughout the world

Anglo-French connections

The geographical closeness of Britain and France has resulted in many links and connections between them. Some of these go back a long time in history. Perhaps the best-known are those links that resulted from the Norman Conquest in 1066.

In Britain today there are many French influences and links which can be recognized – from the makes of cars people drive to the types of food that we can buy (photos **B** and **C**). There are political and economic links between the two countries. Both Britain and France are members of the European Union (see pages 8–9). There are also a number of joint business ventures such as the building and running of the Channel Tunnel, and the development of the European Airbus project which also involves Germany, Spain, the Netherlands and Belgium.

Are the French influenced by Britain?

The short answer to this is yes – the influences are not just one way. For example, a number of English words, such as *weekend*, have been adopted by the French. This is partly due to the fact that English is spoken in the United States of America, and is the main language used in the worlds of information technology and popular culture, particularly the cinema. However, many French people are not happy that English words

C Hypermarkets were popular in France before the first ones were built in Britain

are creeping into their language. There is still a great pride in being French, and the language is a vital part of this 'Frenchness'. There are also regions of France, such as Corsica and Brittany, which have their own language and identity, and this is very important to them.

FACT FILE

Language

French is spoken and used everywhere in France but, like Britain, there are varying accents found in the different regions. There are also some regions and areas which have preserved traditional languages from many centuries ago, when they were not part of the nation of France. These include: Flemish in the far north; Alsatian in Alsace; Breton, (which is similar to Welsh and Cornish) in Brittany; Basque and Catalan in the areas bordering Spain; Provençal in Provence and Corsu in Corsica.

On a global scale about 200 million people speak French. French is spoken in the Val d'Aosta region of north-western Italy and is one of the official languages in the European countries of Belgium, Switzerland and Luxembourg and Canada. This is also the case for over 30 countries in Africa, known as 'Francophone

Africa' which used to be former French colonies. There are also a number of other countries elsewhere in the world which were former colonies of France and where French is still widely spoken e.g. Vietnam and Tahiti. France has a special government ministry, the Ministère de la Francophonie, which deals with the links between France and the French-speaking countries in the world.

Many French are concerned that their language is losing ground to English as a second language. There is also concern about the increase in the number of English words which are used, e.g. le weekend (resulting in a mix known by some as Franglais). Recently the government proposed a law which would have banned many of these words and replaced them with the French equivalents. The law was not passed.

France and the European Union

▶ **Why is France important to the European Union?**

How the European Union started

The idea for the European Union (EU) first came from France in 1945 after the Second World War (photo **A**). The original aim was to build friendship between France and Germany in order to prevent any more wars. One way of doing this was to bring together the economies of France and Germany by setting up the European Coal and Steel Community (ECSC) in 1950. In 1957 France, Germany, Belgium, Italy, Luxembourg and the Netherlands signed the Treaties of Rome, which established the European Economic Community (EEC). In 1967 the EEC and the ECSC joined together to become the European Community (EC). The Maastricht Treaty of 1993 brought in social as well as economic measures. From this time the EC became known as the European Union (map **B**).

A Many parts of France were destroyed or badly damaged during the Second World War

B The growth of the European Union

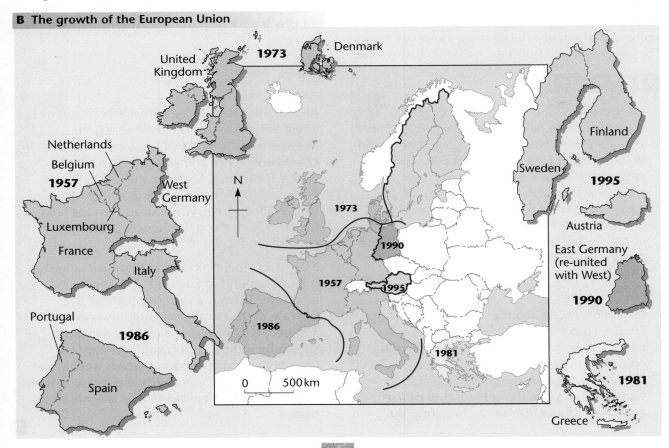

Belonging to the European Union

France still plays an important role in the EU today. It has the second largest economy in the EU and is a major contributor to the economic funds run by the EU. The French like being members of the EU and generally agree with policies e.g. the single European currency (figure **C**). Being a member of the EU affects a country in many ways. There are special trading regulations between EU countries and with countries that do not belong to the Union. Membership means:

- equal job opportunities – any person in any EU country may apply for a job in the other member countries
- passport controls and checks at borders have been cut back
- there is a European Parliament which has representatives (Members of the European Parliament – MEPs) who are voted into office by the people in all member countries.

Another big step towards economic unity was taken at the beginning of 1999 when the first stage of using a single European currency – the euro – was introduced. This development is called the European Monetary Union (EMU). The French and British governments have taken different views on this – the British have chosen not to join, at least for the time being.

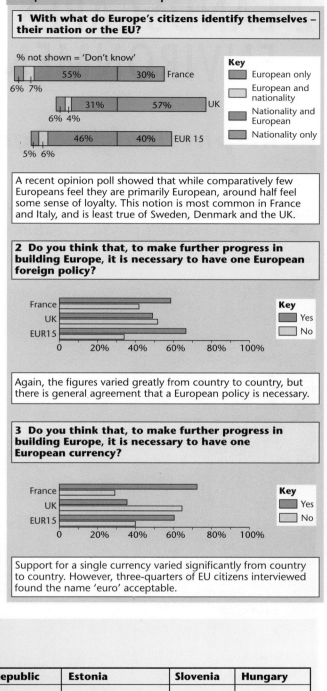

C Opinions on membership of the EU

1 With what do Europe's citizens identify themselves – their nation or the EU?

% not shown = 'Don't know'

France: 6% 7% 55% 30%
UK: 6% 4% 31% 57%
EUR 15: 5% 6% 46% 40%

Key
- European only
- European and nationality
- Nationality and European
- Nationality only

A recent opinion poll showed that while comparatively few Europeans feel they are primarily European, around half feel some sense of loyalty. This notion is most common in France and Italy, and is least true of Sweden, Denmark and the UK.

2 Do you think that, to make further progress in building Europe, it is necessary to have one European foreign policy?

France, UK, EUR15 — scale 0 to 100%

Key
- Yes
- No

Again, the figures varied greatly from country to country, but there is general agreement that a European policy is necessary.

3 Do you think that, to make further progress in building Europe, it is necessary to have one European currency?

France, UK, EUR15 — scale 0 to 100%

Key
- Yes
- No

Support for a single currency varied significantly from country to country. However, three-quarters of EU citizens interviewed found the name 'euro' acceptable.

FACT FILE

Future expansion of the European Union

There are a number of countries which have applied, or are planning to apply, to join the European Union (EU). The first 'wave' is due to join from January 2002 and a brief profile of them is given in this table:

Country	Poland	Cyprus	Czech Republic	Estonia	Slovenia	Hungary
Population	38 million	752 000	10 million	1.5 million	2 million	10 million
GDP per head (£)	4004	8750	7328	2778	7688	4687
Unemployment (%)	10.5	3.1	5.2	4.6	14.8	10.4
Big issues	25% work on farms	island is divided between Greeks and Turks	pollution; foreigners buying land	special trade agreement with Latvia and Lithuania	none	foreigners buying land

The next 'wave' will join from January 2010, and may include: Bulgaria, Romania, Slovakia, Latvia, Lithuania, Turkey, Malta, Russia, and Ukraine.

2 LANDSCAPES AND THE ENVIRONMENT

The physical background

▶ What are France's main physical features?
▶ How do France's physical features affect the country's land use and economy?

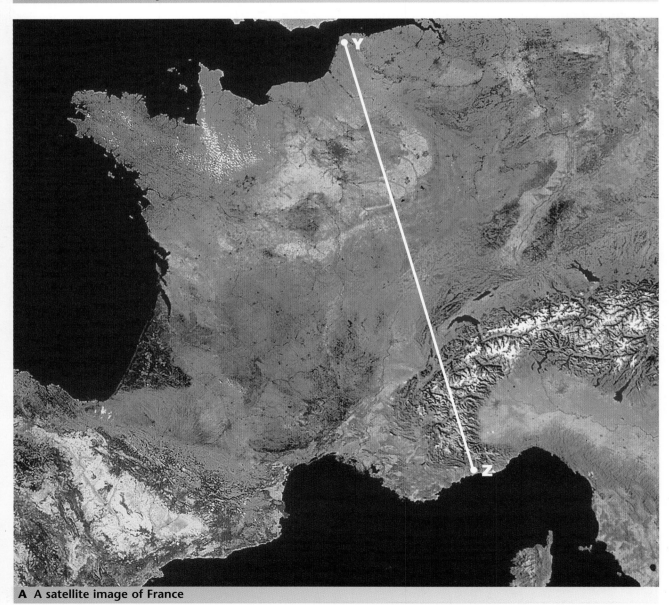

A A satellite image of France

B River Lot

C Brittany coastline

Highland areas

About 60 per cent of France is less than 250 metres above sea level, but there are distinctive highland areas:

- The French Alps include Mont Blanc. At 4807m, it is the highest peak in Europe.
- The Jura Mountains are to the north of the Alps. They are formed of limestone, and their highest point is 1723m.
- The Pyrénées run from the Atlantic Ocean to the Mediterranean Sea. The highest point is 3404m.
- The Massif Central is in the middle of France. Formed about 300 million years ago it covers about 15 per cent of the country. It is famous for extinct volcanoes, e.g. the Puy de Dôme which is 1465m high. Some of France's main rivers start in this area.

Rivers and coasts

France has five large river systems: the Seine, the Loire, the Rhône, the Rhine (partly) and the Garonne (which includes the Dordogne, the Lot (photo **B**) and the Tarn).

The 3200km long coastline is varied and includes chalk cliffs in Normandy, sandy beaches along the Atlantic coast (photo **C**) and rocky beaches along parts of the Mediterranean coast.

Physical features and human activity

France is more than twice the size of the UK in area, but the total population is similar in size. About 15 per cent of the population lives in the Paris region. There are large areas of the rest of France with very few people. Settlements, farming, transport routes and industry are mainly found in the lowland areas because it is easier to build here. However, the beautiful scenery and winter sports of the mountains attract many tourists. The beaches also attract tourists. Some coastal parts of France have important fishing industries.

FACT FILE

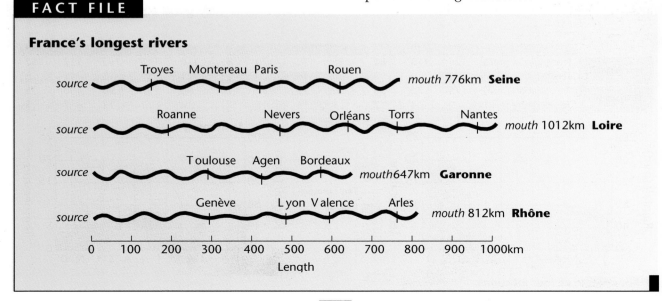

France's longest rivers

| source | Troyes | Montereau | Paris | | Rouen | *mouth* 776km **Seine** |

| source | Roanne | | Nevers | Orléans | Torrs | Nantes | *mouth* 1012km **Loire** |

| source | Toulouse | Agen | Bordeaux | *mouth* 647km **Garonne** |

| source | Genève | | Lyon | Valence | Arles | *mouth* 812km **Rhône** |

0   100   200   300   400   500   600   700   800   900   1000km

Length

Climate and vegetation

▶ What are the features and the causes of France's climate?
▶ How does the climate affect vegetation?
▶ How does the climate affect people?

France lies between latitudes 42°N and 52°N on the western side of the **landmass** of Europe and Asia (Eurasia). This position means that France generally has mild winters, although there are differences between north and south, and between lowland and mountainous areas (map A and figure B). The weather patterns of France are caused by the influences of the Atlantic Ocean and the Mediterranean Sea, the continental landmass and the mountains (figure C). These influences vary in importance and this causes a variety of climates. For example, the area along the south coast has a **Mediterranean type climate** whilst the area to the north-west, around Strasbourg, has a **continental type climate**.

Natural vegetation

As a result of the different climates, there is a variety of natural vegetation in France (map A). Certain plants and trees will grow in an area depending on the amount and type of **precipitation**, on the **range of temperature**, and the soil. In fact, there is very little natural vegetation left in France as most of it has been cleared for farming, settlement, industries, and so on.

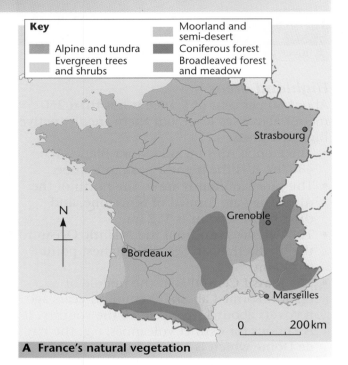

Key

Alpine and tundra	Moorland and semi-desert
Evergreen trees and shrubs	Coniferous forest
	Broadleaved forest and meadow

A France's natural vegetation

Climate and people

The great variety of climates in France means that it is possible to sunbathe and ski in different parts of the country at the same time of year. This is very good for the tourist

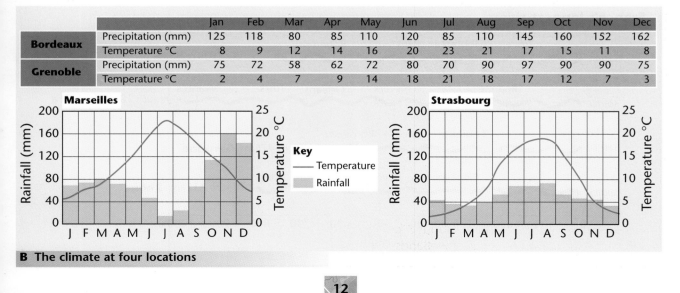

		Jan	Feb	Mar	Apr	May	Jun	Jul	Aug	Sep	Oct	Nov	Dec
Bordeaux	Precipitation (mm)	125	118	80	85	110	120	85	110	145	160	152	162
	Temperature °C	8	9	12	14	16	20	23	21	17	15	11	8
Grenoble	Precipitation (mm)	75	72	58	62	72	80	70	90	97	90	90	75
	Temperature °C	2	4	7	9	14	18	21	18	17	12	7	3

Key
— Temperature
▨ Rainfall

B The climate at four locations

industry, as there is always a range of attractions for tourists throughout the year. The variety of climatic types also means that there are many different types of farming in France. For example, grapes need lots of sunshine and heat so they are not a major crop in northern France. Dairy cattle need lower temperatures and pasture so are important in central and northern France.

There are a few effects of climate that are not so good for human activities.

- Some regions in the south of France may suffer from **drought**, particularly during the summer months.
- Parts of the south are affected by a cold dry wind called the **Mistral**, which blows down the valley of the Rhône for about 100 days each year. The risk is worst during the spring when it is strong enough to damage crops and buildings.
- In the mountainous regions snow may block roads and railways or, occasionally, **avalanches** may cause problems for settlements.

SEA
- Warms slowly during summer.
- Cools slowly during winter.
- Warm ocean current passes close to west coast of France in the winter.

RELIEF
- Temperature drops approx. 0.6 °C every 100m.
- Causes formation of relief rainfall in path of prevailing wind.

CONTINENTAL LANDMASS
- Warms quickly during the summer.
- Cools quickly during the winter.

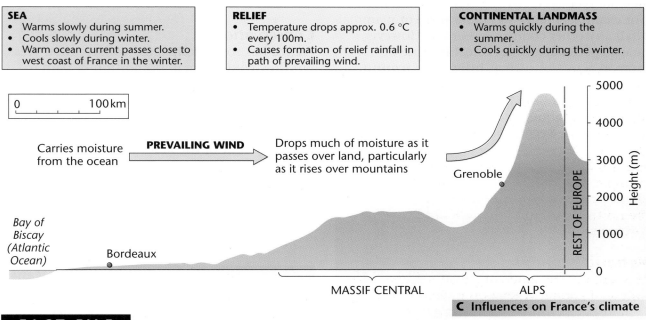

C Influences on France's climate

FACT FILE

Forests and wetlands
There are 14 million hectares of forest in France which cover approximately one-fifth of the country. The most common types of trees are beech, oak and pine. The forests are managed by the Office Nationale des Forêts (ONF). However they are not protected, and French environmentalists criticise the ONF for giving the commercial sale of timber far more importance than conservation. In the hotter, drier areas of France summer forest fires are a serious hazard. Large areas are burnt every year, often because someone carelessly dropped a match or cigarette end. The forests in the north have been affected by **acid rain** and many of the trees are dying.

More than two million hectares, about 3 per cent of French territory, is made up of wetlands. These are very productive ecosystems which support a large number of birds, reptiles and amphibians. However, only 4 per cent of these wetlands are protected. Many are being damaged, or even destroyed, by human activities such as agriculture, industry and tourism.

The natural environment and people

Habitats under threat

There are many different types of animals and plants in France because of the great variety of climate types and environments found there. For example, France has more types of mammal than any other country in Europe. However, many species are under threat because of human activities such as **intensive farming** (photo A), hunting and tourism. In many places these activities have led to the clearing of natural vegetation, so today very little of it is left. Once the vegetation disappears, most wildlife cannot survive. Wildlife that has already been wiped out include the Pyrénées ibex and the Corsican deer. Others on the endangered list include brown bears and wolves.

Conservation

France has some designated conservation areas, but they cover a small proportion of land in relation to the size and population of the country. The different types of conservation area are:

- *Parcs nationaux* (national parks) cover about 0.7 per cent of the land. There are 6 of them, but they are all under 1000km². Most of them are in the mountains of the Alps and the Pyrénées. Generally there are no, or very few, people living in them, and camping is restricted here. Hunting, dogs and vehicles are banned from them.

A Intensive agriculture in the Ile de France

B The Parc National des Cévennes

PARC NATIONAL DES CÉVENNES

**Parc National des Cévennes
(photo B and map C)**
It is in the south of the Massif Central and covers 910km². Its many different habitats include:
- the granite mountain of Mont Lozère (1699m), covered with heather, blueberries and peat bogs
- many valleys in which sweet chestnut trees were planted back in the Middle Ages.

The park was created in 1970 to conserve these habitats. They had been threatened in the past by people trying to make a living by logging and grazing livestock. Today very few people live in the area. It is illegal to build new houses within the park, and all renovations of old buildings must fit in with the local architecture. Some of the wildlife, such as red deer and vultures, which had disappeared from the area, has been re-introduced as part of the park's conservation plans.

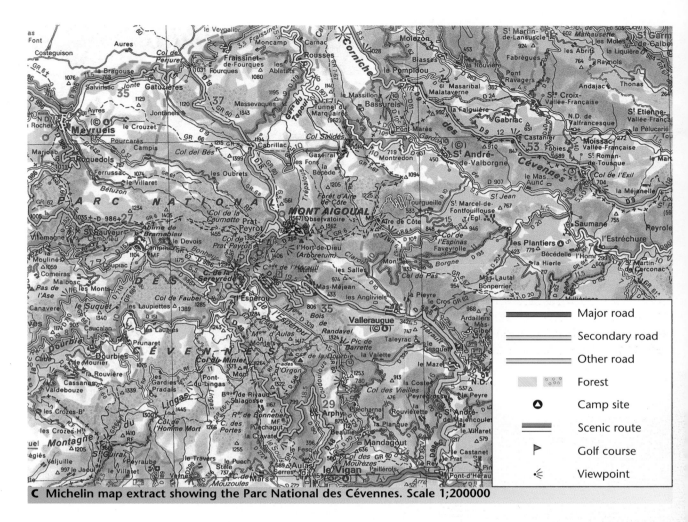

C Michelin map extract showing the Parc National des Cévennes. Scale 1;200000

Legend:
- Major road
- Secondary road
- Other road
- Forest
- Camp site
- Scenic route
- Golf course
- Viewpoint

- *Parcs naturels regionaux* (regional parks) cover 7 per cent of the land. There are 26 of them. People live within these although they are generally in areas where the population is declining, for example parts of the Massif Central and Corsica. They aim to protect ecosystems and to encourage economic development, including tourism.
- *Réserves naturelles* (nature reserves) – there are nearly 100 of these but they are all small.

FACT FILE

Human activity in the Alps

In the Alps, permanent snow cover during the winter months and the steep slopes attract large numbers of tourists, and there are many purpose-built resorts for them. The ski industry brings much money into these areas and provides jobs. This means that local people may be able to stay rather than migrate to find work. However, there are problems for the environment. Trees are cleared for ski slopes, hotels and other facilities. The delicate balance of the environment is then damaged, resulting in increased run-off, more soil erosion and the removal of natural buffers and protection barriers. This leads to greater risks of avalanches, landslips and flooding. These problems are likely to get worse as tourist numbers increase and tourist developments spread. Steps are being taken by the French to protect the Alpine environment – there are three national parks – but it is difficult to balance conservation with economic needs.

Human activity and the Camargue

▶ **What are the natural and human features of the Camargue?**
▶ **What conservation measures have been taken?**
▶ **Why is the Camargue under threat from human activity?**

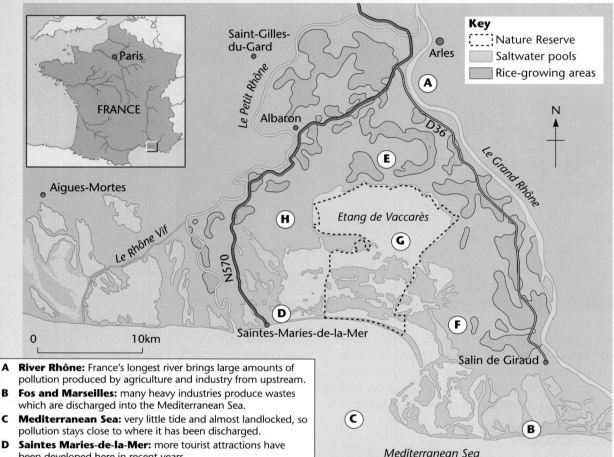

Key
- ⌐¬ Nature Reserve
- ▢ Saltwater pools
- ▢ Rice-growing areas

A **River Rhône:** France's longest river brings large amounts of pollution produced by agriculture and industry from upstream.

B **Fos and Marseilles:** many heavy industries produce wastes which are discharged into the Mediterranean Sea.

C **Mediterranean Sea:** very little tide and almost landlocked, so pollution stays close to where it has been discharged.

D **Saintes Maries-de-la-Mer:** more tourist attractions have been developed here in recent years.

E **Rice growing areas:** water from the Rhône, and high temperatures, give the conditions needed for rice to be grown.

F **Salt production pools:** found in the southern parts where the amount of salt in the water and soil is high.

G **Nature Reserve:** created in 1928, an area of 135 km^2 where people are not allowed.

H **Regional Park:** created in 1970, an area of 850 km^2 where access is allowed but controlled.

A Physical and human features of the Camargue

Natural features

The Camargue is a **delta** covering about 780 km^2 (map **A**). It was formed by the River Rhône, where it meets the Mediterranean Sea. The Camargue is mainly a wetland with water channels, salt marshes and inland lakes, and

B The landscape and birds of the Camargue

some dry land in the north. It is famous for the many birds that can be seen here, including huge flocks of flamingos (photo **B**).

Living on the Camargue

The Camargue is well-known for white horses and black bulls which graze the marshes. Raising bulls for bull-fighting is a tradition here. There are about 9000 people living in the Camargue, and most farm the land. About 40 per cent of the Camargue is farmed. Much is drained for livestock, pasture or irrigated for rice and wheat. Recently, tourism has become very important to the local economy. Over a million tourists visit every year.

Conflicts and pressures

The Camargue is a very important natural environment. Its habitat is fragile and easily damaged by human activities. Steps have been taken to protect and conserve it (map **A**). Despite these measures, the Camargue is still threatened by human activities. Until recently it was difficult to get to, but now tourists can get there easily by motorway and by rail. Tourists use a lot of water and produce huge amounts of waste which ends up in the water of the area. Pollution also comes from agriculture and industries (figure **C**). Planners

C A satellite image showing around the Rhône delta. Worst affected areas are red.

must decide how to balance economic prosperity with conservation. The history of rice production shows that it can cost a lot to do this. In some ways it is good to grow rice in the Camargue. It benefits the natural environment because irrigation for the crop keeps a good balance between fresh and salt water. Between 1960 and 1980 it was cheaper to buy rice from abroad so rice production dropped and the soil in parts of the Camargue became too salty for any plants to grow. In 1981 it was obvious that the environment was suffering, so the government decided to subsidise farmers so that they would grow rice again.

FACT FILE

The Rhône delta

As the River Rhône approaches the sea it divides into a number of channels called distributaries. The two main distributaries, the Grand Rhône and the Petit Rhône, enclose a triangle of land between them which forms the delta of the River Rhône. The Rhône transports large volumes of silt, sand and pebbles, called its load. Where the river enters the Mediterranean Sea, its speed is slowed down and so it drops its load. The delta has been built up by the dropped load over a long period of time. It does not get washed away by the sea because the Mediterranean has a very small tidal range and the coastline is not affected by strong waves or currents. There is also relatively shallow water at the mouth of the river.

The Rhône delta is an example of an arcuate, or fan-shaped delta. There are two other types of delta – a bird's foot delta, e.g. the River

Mississippi, USA, and a cuspate delta, e.g. the River Ebro, Spain. Bird's foot deltas form when the silt from the river is deposited a long way out to sea along the edges of the river channels. Cuspate deltas form when one major river channel carries most of the silt into the sea. (Cuspate means shaped like a tooth.)

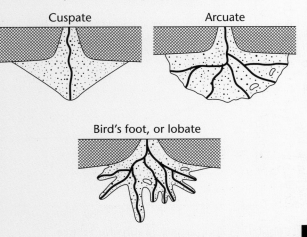

3 POPULATION, PEOPLE AND CITIES

Population change

▶ How and why has France's population changed?
▶ What effects will this have on France?

Population change

A change in the total population of a country depends partly on the balance between **birth rate** and **death rate**. The difference between the two rates gives a **natural increase** or decrease. In 1998 France had a birth rate of 13 and a death rate of 9 (figure **B**). The population total can also change because of **migration** between countries.

The change in a country's population is called its **demographic transition**. Economically developed countries, like France, have been through several stages in their demographic transition:

- first stage – birth rate and death rate are high, so total population does not change
- second stage – death rate falls, so the population increases rapidly
- third stage – birth rate starts to fall but the population growth remains high
- fourth stage – both birth and death rates are low so there is a slow growth, or none at all (this is called zero population growth).

	1950	1960	1970	1980	1990	2000 (predicted)
Birth rate	20	18	16	15	13	12
Death rate	13	11	11	11	10	9

B Birth and death rates (per 1000) in France, 1950–2000

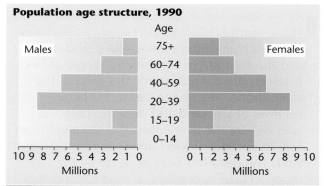

Population age structure, 1990

Population age structure: projections 2015 (millions)

Age	Males	Females
0–14	5.49	5.23
15–19	1.90	1.81
20–39	7.97	7.78
40–59	7.98	8.24
60–74	3.50	4.09
75+	1.60	2.86

C Population structures: 1990 and 2015

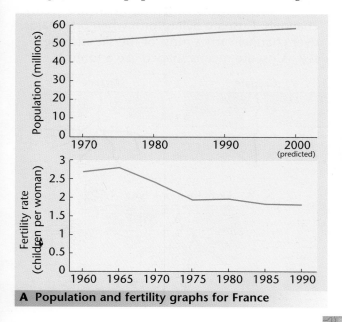

A Population and fertility graphs for France

In some European countries, like Italy, it looks as if there is now a fifth stage, when the birth rate falls lower than the death rate. This leads to a natural decrease.

Death rate, birth rate and life expectancy

The death rate has fallen in France this century because of better medical care. This means that fewer babies die and people live longer.

The birth rate has fallen for many reasons. Birth control means couples can choose how many children to have. Fewer children mean there is more money available to spend on them, and on other things that make life more comfortable. More women go out to work, and some may choose to have a career rather than children.

The effects of population change

The French government is worried about the fall in birth rate and the increase in life expectancy.

- The fall in birth rate means not enough children are born to replace the present population. The number of children born to each woman is called the **fertility rate** (figure **A**). The fertility rate of a country needs to be 2.1 to replace the population: below this the total population will decrease. It also means that there will be fewer young people

D Children at a daycare nursery in Paris

to work. This may then lead to higher wages, putting France at a disadvantage with other countries where wages are lower. Another problem is that fewer workers mean less tax is being paid. Less tax then means less money for social services like health care.

- The increase in life expectancy means there will be more elderly people in the population (figure **C**). They will need more health care and pensions. The government has a serious problem paying for these if there is also a drop in the number of young people. The **dependency ratio** is the balance between those who earn a living and those who are too young or too old to work.

FACT FILE

French population trends

Although the level of natural increase in the French population has been higher than that of the UK, Germany and Italy, there is still concern that not enough babies are being born to keep the population growing. The increase in the number of those over the age of 59 has slowed down, from 1.6 million in the 1980s to 1.1 million in the 1990s. However, this slowing down is only temporary because people born in the 'baby boom' between 1946–1973 will be reaching the age of 60 from 2006 onwards. By 2010 it is predicted that the 60+ population will make up 23 per cent of the total French population.

Birth and death rates in EU countries (per 1000)

	Birth rate	**Death rate**
Austria	12	12
Belgium	12	12
Denmark	11	11
Finland	12	10
France	**13**	**10**
Germany	11	12
Greece	12	10
Ireland	18	8
Italy	11	11
Luxembourg	12	11
Netherlands	13	9
Portugal	13	10
Spain	13	9
Sweden	13	12
UK	14	12

Migration into France

▶ Why do people move to France?

The history of migration into France

Over the past 150 years France has received more **immigrants** than other European countries (figure **A**). Between 1850 and the First World War, 4.3 million arrived, followed by 3 million in the time before the Second World War. The main reason at these times was that France was in need of workers, particularly after the First World War when so many young men were killed. Most of the migrants at this time came from other European countries, especially Italy, Switzerland, Belgium, Spain and Poland. After the Second World War several million more migrated to France for the same reason.

During the late 1950s and early 1960s the French colonial empire collapsed. Over one million people came to France from North, West and Central Africa and from Indo-China, particularly Vietnam. In 1974 a law was passed to stop large-scale immigration. However, migrants already living in France were allowed to bring their families to join them. Between 1982 and 1990, 450 000 people moved to France for this reason. In 1994 another law was passed, making it much harder for anyone, even family members, to come into France.

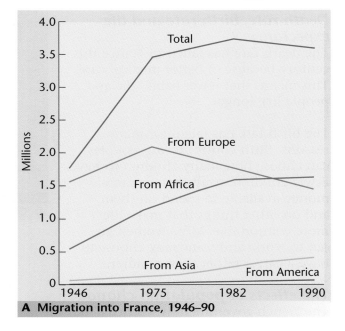

A Migration into France, 1946–90

B Movement of migrants into France, 1990

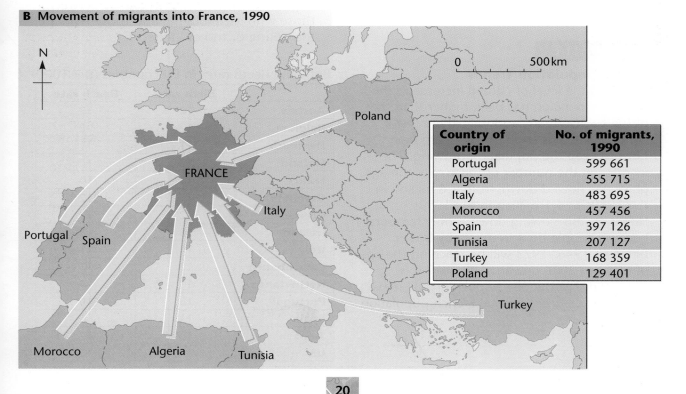

Country of origin	No. of migrants, 1990
Portugal	599 661
Algeria	555 715
Italy	483 695
Morocco	457 456
Spain	397 126
Tunisia	207 127
Turkey	168 359
Poland	129 401

	France	Algeria	Morocco
Birth rate (per 1000 people)	13	35	33
Death rate (per 1000 people)	9	7	8
Infant mortality (deaths per 1000 births)	6	61	68
Population aged 0-14	20%	44%	41%
Life expectancy (years): male	75	65	62
female	83	67	65
Urban population	74%	45%	49%
GNP per person (US$)	24 990	2 170	900
Persons per TV	2.7	13.9	19.4
Persons per phone	1.6	27.4	69.2
Person per car	2.5	33.4	44.2
Literacy	99%	43%	62%
UN Human Development Index	0.93	0.60	0.48

C Population, economy and quality of life: France, Algeria and Morocco

D Different cultural influences

Migration from the EU and North Africa

Many of the most recent migrants have come from the European Union and North Africa (map **B**). For members of EU countries it is becoming easier to move to another EU country, and the aim is to eventually allow free movement of people within the Union. People come from North African countries such as Algeria and Tunisia because they are near to France, and also because many of their people speak French. This is left over from the past when these countries were part of the French colonial empire.

Present-day situation

Migrants and their families make up 4 per cent of the total population and 10 per cent of the working population. Nearly two-thirds live in the regions of Paris (Ile de France), Rhône-Alpes and Provence-Alpes-Côte d'Azur, bringing a range of different cultural influences with them (photo **D**). There are a number of issues to do with migration into France that the government has to deal with:

- Some people in France do not want migrants from outside the EU coming into France. This has led to an increase in racism and the problems connected with it.
- There is some illegal immigration taking place across the Mediterranean. This has been called the 'Mediterranean Rio Grande'. This is because the Mediterranean divides the economically developed countries of Europe from the economically developing countries of Africa, in the same way that the Rio Grande River divides the USA from Mexico.
- Soon France will have a shortage of workers. This is because it has an ageing population. In the past this kind of shortage has been solved by inviting in migrants from other countries.

FACT FILE

Labour market characteristics for the Mediterranean area

Country	% Total activity rate 1990	% Female activity rate 1990	% Unemployment 1990	% active population engaged in:						GNP p/c 1991 (US$)
				Agriculture		Industry		Services		
				1970	1990	1970	1990	1970	1990	
France	45.8	33.8	10.3	13.6	6.9	39.3	30.3	47.1	62.8	17 830
Italy	40.5	23.6	11.3	20.2	9.0	39.5	32.4	40.3	58.6	15 150
Greece	38.2	19.5	7.7	40.8	24.5	25.0	27.4	34.2	48.2	5340
Spain	36.3	32.8	16.3	27.1	11.8	35.5	33.4	37.4	54.8	9150
Morocco	31.8	10.8	12.0	57.7	45.6	17.0	25.0	25.4	29.4	900
Algeria	22.8	3.5	22.7	47.4	23.5	21.3	31.7	31.4	44.8	2170
Tunisia	32.8	12.6	16.8	42.1	26.2	25.3	33.3	32.5	34.3	1260
Egypt	27.7	4.7	14.0	51.9	38.2	16.5	18.9	31.6	42.9	630
Turkey	43.3	30.4	10.1	70.7	50.0	11.9	21.0	17.4	29.0	1360

Where people live in France – 1

▶ How is the population distributed in France?
▶ Why are some areas more densely populated than others?
▶ What population movements are there within France?

Where people live in France

We can use two geographical terms to talk about where people live. **Population density** is the number of people for every square kilometre (km²). It is an average figure for an area and so cannot show that particular places may have more people than other places. For example, the Ile de France has over 151 people per km² (map A) but, within the region, Paris has nearly 900 per km². The spread of where people live is called the **population distribution**. France has great regional variations in the distribution of its population.

Factors affecting where people live

Many factors influence where people live, including relief, climate, resources and economic development. The areas with fewest people are the mountains where farming is difficult and access may also cause problems. Areas with the densest population tend to be those with flatter, low-lying land where farming and the building of settlements and communications are much easier.

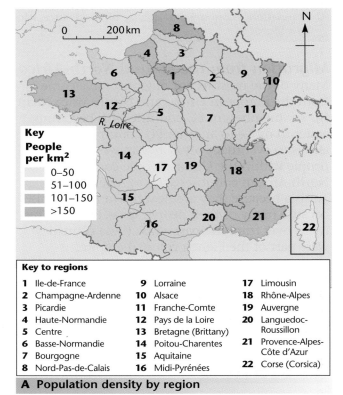

Key
People per km²
0–50
51–100
101–150
>150

Key to regions

1 Ile-de-France	9 Lorraine	17 Limousin
2 Champagne-Ardenne	10 Alsace	18 Rhône-Alpes
3 Picardie	11 Franche-Comte	19 Auvergne
4 Haute-Normandie	12 Pays de la Loire	20 Languedoc-Roussillon
5 Centre	13 Bretagne (Brittany)	21 Provence-Alpes-Côte d'Azur
6 Basse-Normandie	14 Poitou-Charentes	22 Corse (Corsica)
7 Bourgogne	15 Aquitaine	
8 Nord-Pas-de-Calais	16 Midi-Pyrénées	

A Population density by region

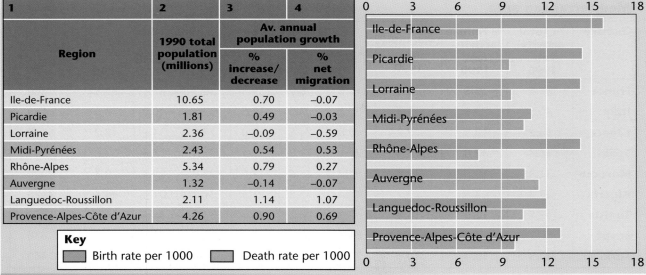

Region	1990 total population (millions)	Av. annual population growth	
		% increase/ decrease	% net migration
Ile-de-France	10.65	0.70	–0.07
Picardie	1.81	0.49	–0.03
Lorraine	2.36	–0.09	–0.59
Midi-Pyrénées	2.43	0.54	0.53
Rhône-Alpes	5.34	0.79	0.27
Auvergne	1.32	–0.14	–0.07
Languedoc-Roussillon	2.11	1.14	1.07
Provence-Alpes-Côte d'Azur	4.26	0.90	0.69

Key
Birth rate per 1000   Death rate per 1000

B Population profiles, and birth and death rates of selected regions

Population changes within France

The population of each region may change over a period of time. **Natural population changes** in regions may be caused by a difference between the birth rate and the death rate. One example of a region with a natural population gain is Picardie, in the north.

Population changes in regions may also be caused by people migrating from one region to another. The number of people living in mountainous and rural areas has been declining since the 1950s. Many are moving to regions with lower relief, larger settlements and better communications (figure **B**).

The last two censuses have shown another general trend: people moving southwards within the country. Generally regions south of the River Loire are attracting more people. **Net migration** is the number of people moving in balanced against those moving out. Regions towards the south, e.g. Languedoc-Roussillon, have a net migration gain (photo **C**). Many northern regions have a net migration loss, e.g. Picardie. This would need to be taken into account for the complete picture of population change.

Reasons why people move

People are moving within France mainly because of changes in employment. There are now fewer jobs available in farming and heavy industries. New jobs have been created in high-tech industries and tourism. Some of the mountainous regions in France have a strong tourist industry which encourages people to continue living there.

C Many people move to the region of Languedoc-Roussillon

Differences in the growth of towns and cities

Although there is an increase in the total urban population of France, not all urban areas have grown at the same rate. In recent years, the largest cities (over 200 000) and the smallest towns (under 20 000) have grown the fastest. There has been a particularly big surge in the growth of the largest cities between 1982–90 compared to earlier. This is thought to be because the most thriving industries (e.g. high tech) prefer to locate in large urban areas which offer a range of facilities.

Size of town/city (thousands)	Annual growth rate (%)	
	1975-82	1982-90
Paris conurbation	0.05	0.50
200-2000	0.16	0.38
100-199	0.21	0.19
50-99	0.26	0.25
20-49	0.26	0.24
10-19	0.62	0.41
5-9	0.89	0.54
2-5	1.0	0.62

Regional population changes

Between 1980–90 the region of Languedoc-Roussillon had a net migration gain of 215 900, whilst over the same period, Picardie had a net migration loss of 3700. The diagrams below show that there are differences between the two regions, but also similarities.

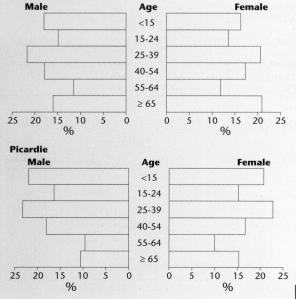

▶ How has the population in rural and urban areas been changing?

▶ In what ways has this change affected rural and urban areas?

Growth of the urban population

In France, 74 per cent of the population live in towns and cities (**urban areas**). The rest live in villages and farms (**rural areas**). The last census carried out in France showed that people are still moving from rural areas into urban areas (figure **A**). This means that the population of France will become even more concentrated into urban areas.

A Rural/urban population change

Cities of more than 250 000 in 1990 * French part	Population 1993 (thousands)	% change, 1982–90
1+ million		
Paris	9318	4.0
Lyons	1262	3.3
Marseilles	1230	–2.2
500 000 – 1 million		
Lille	959	1.5
Bordeaux	696	7.0
Toulouse	650	12.4
250 000 – 500 000		
Nice	516	5.8
Nantes	496	5.8
Toulon	437	6.6
Grenoble	404	2.0
Strasbourg*	388	4.0
Rouen	380	0.1
Valenciennes*	338	–4.0
Grasse-Cannes-Antibes	335	13.6
Nancy	329	1.3
Lens	323	_1.2
Saint-Etienne	313	–1.3
Tours	272	3.4
Béthune	260	0.5
Clermont-Ferrand	254	–0.8
Le Havre	254	–0.4

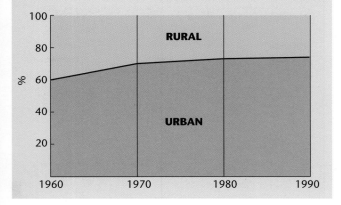

Differences in urban areas

The term 'urban area' includes both towns as small as 5000 and cities with more than one million people. The details of exactly where people are moving are quite complex. People moving from a rural area are more likely to go to a small town than to a city. At the same time there are people moving from small towns into cities. Nowadays they will probably move to the suburbs, which are gaining population, whilst the centre is losing people.

Moving from the countryside to the town

Madeleine (aged 10): I do not want to leave here (photo **B**) as it has been my home since I was born. My grandparents have lived here all their lives and their parents too. Our family has had a small piece of land to farm for as long as anyone can remember. It's always been too small to make enough money to live on, but now my dad can't get the extra work on other farms because farms have got smaller or machines are now used to do the jobs my granddad used to do. My dad has got a job in a bottled-water factory in Clermont-Ferrand (photo **C**). I don't really want to live in a town – I like the open space here. But my best friend and her family moved there last year and it's been lonely since then. Also, it will be nice not to have to travel so far to school.

Moving from a small town to a city

Davide (aged 14): We are about to move to Lyons. My dad has got a job in the headquarters of a big computer company there. My mum is pleased because she will have a better choice of jobs there. We have lived here in Annecy for about ten years. The town is big enough to have lots of facilities but small enough so that you can get to know lots of people who live here. I suppose that will be one of the biggest differences between here and Lyons. At least we're going to live in the suburbs (photo **D**) where it should be easier to get to know people. The centre is not too far away, although we've heard that the traffic can be bad (photo **E**). I've also heard that there are things for people my age to do – that will be an improvement on here anyway!

B Rural area in the Auvergne region

C Centre of Clermont-Ferrand

D Suburbs of Lyons

E The centre of Lyons

FACT FILE

Clermont-Ferrand and Michelin tyres

Clermont-Ferrand dominates the region of the Auvergne. It has grown from a settlement of 42 000 in 1876 to a **conurbation** with a population of over 360 000 in 1990. The reason for its development over this time is the existence of the Michelin tyre company. This was started by two brothers who went from making rubber toys to bicycle tyres, and car tyres over a period of 20 years: by 1895 they were well known in the car tyre market.

Michelin is now a multi-national company with the largest share of the world's tyre market. At its peak, in the 1980s, Michelin employed one in three of the working population in Clermont-Ferrand. Today there are still nearly 20 000 employed in the five factories in the

city (out of 49 000 employees in France and 117 000 worldwide). Despite its global importance Michelin has stayed in Clermont-Ferrand because the local workforce have the skills needed.

The company has always invested in the community. In the late 19th century it built 'colonies' for the employees, similar to the 'garden cities' being developed in England at that time by Ebenezer Howard. More recently the company has helped to establish a second technological university in Clermont-Ferrand.

Paris 1

▶ **How do different groups of people view Paris?**

▶ **How is the Paris region defined?**

Definitions of Paris

When people talk about Paris they could mean three different things:

- the city of Paris, which has a population of 2.1 million, or
- the conurbation of Paris, also known as the Paris region, which has a population of over 9 million, or
- the region of the Ile de France which stretches up to 100km away from the actual city and has 20 per cent of France's total population.

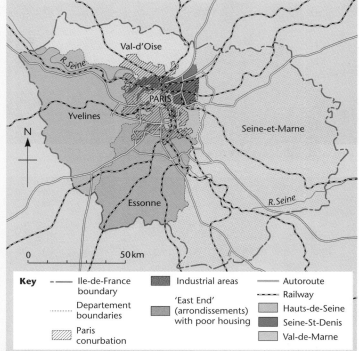

A The Paris region

Key

- — — Ile-de-France boundary
- ⋯⋯ Departement boundaries
- ▨ Paris conurbation
- ▓ Industrial areas
- ▨ 'East End' (arrondissements) with poor housing
- ═ Autoroute
- ┈ Railway
- ▨ Hauts-de-Seine
- ▨ Seine-St-Denis
- ▨ Val-de-Marne

Images of Paris

'Paris has just about exhausted the superlatives that can be applied to cities...... Notre Dame and the Eiffel Tower have been described countless times. But what travel writers have been unable to capture is the grandness and even magic of strolling along the city's broad avenues (**boulevards**), which lead from impressive public buildings and exceptional museums to parks, gardens and esplanades galore. With the Metro, all this and more is readily accessible – you can whizz around under the crowds and traffic and pop up wherever you choose!'

Lonely Planet Guide to France, 1994

'The two major inner city problems are traffic congestion and overcrowding. The transport system has to cope with 3 million commuters, of which 35% travel by private car, for whom the main problem is parking. This seems strange when considering the wide boulevards but these have to cope with dense traffic flows, and kerb-side parking is highly restricted. The Metro, the underground system, is not as extensive as that of London, and only goes as far as the inner suburban ring, at which point commuters travelling to the suburbs have to transfer to bus.'

The New Europe: into the 1990s, 1990

Key

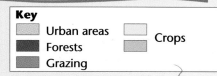

- ▨ Urban areas
- ▓ Forests
- ▨ Grazing
- ▨ Crops

B Satellite image of Paris and surrounding area

Quality of life (photo C)

Paris is the capital city of France and is known throughout the world as a centre of commerce and culture. Commercial organizations are attracted to Paris because it offers a lot of advantages, e.g. good communications with other parts of France and Europe, many other companies to do business with, and a highly skilled work-force. People like to live in Paris because it offers good jobs, lots of facilities such as cafés and shops, and interesting places to visit such as the Louvre art gallery. However, being such a large and fast-growing city brings problems as well, for example traffic congestion and overcrowding (see pages 28–29).

C Life in Paris is a mixture of benefits and drawbacks

D The Paris region: some facts and figures

	Population			Unemploy-ment	Employment			GDP per person
	Thousands, 1990	People/km² 1990	% change 1980–90	% 1990	% agriculture 1990	% industry 1990	% services 1990	Europe=100 1989
Paris	2 154	21 537	−2.6	9.4	0	16	84	318
Seine-et-Marne	1 074	182	27.4	6.8	3	33	64	95
Yvelines	1 305	567	12.6	5.1	1	32	67	104
Essonne	1 083	601	12.0	5.3	1	29	70	96
Hauts-de-Seine	1 392	6 960	−0.6	5.8	0	36	64	236
Seine-St-Denis	1 380	6 902	4.6	9.2	0	32	68	108
Val-de-Marne	1 216	6 077	1.5	6.3	0	24	76	112
Val-d'Oise	1 047	872	17.2	7.1	1	27	72	93
Ile-de-France	10 651	887	6.6	7.2	1	26	74	162
FRANCE	56 597	104	5.3	8.7	6	30	64	109

FACT FILE

Population and employment in the Ile de France region

Population growth in the Ile de France.

	1975	1990	1995
Paris	2 299,8	2 154	2 131,0
Seine-et-Marne	755,8	1 074	1 179,8
Yvelines	1 082,3	1 305	1 368,0
Essonne	923,1	1 083	1 146,9
Hauts-de-Seine	1 438,9	1 392	1 405,3
Seine-Saint-Denis	1 322,1	1 380	1 406,2
Val-de Marne	1 215,7	1 216	1 236,0
Val-d'Oise	840,9	1 047	1 108,6
Ile de France	**9 878,6**	**10 651**	**10 981,8**

Employment structure (%).

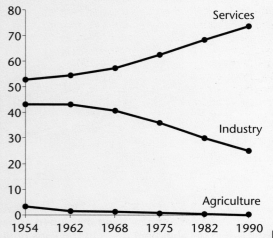

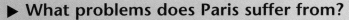

▶ **What problems does Paris suffer from?**
▶ **How are these problems being tackled?**

Urban problems

Problems of traffic congestion and overcrowding mentioned on page 27 affect both the region and the city. Planners have come up with **urban development plans**, for both the region around Paris and the city itself, which tackle these problems.

Urban development in the Ile-de-France (map A)

Until the 1960s, the growth of the conurbation was very chaotic. In 1965 five **new towns** were planned to:

* prevent the city of Paris from spreading outwards and so completely taking over the countryside, and
* encourage urban growth to be more balanced.

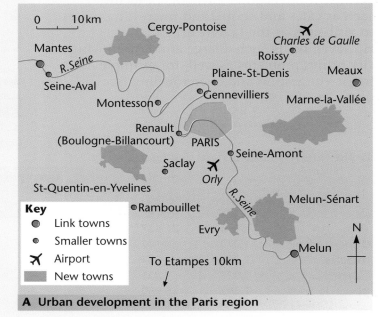

A Urban development in the Paris region

These new towns – Cergy-Pontoise (photo **B**), Evry, Marne-la-Vallée, Melun-Sénart and Saint-Quentin-en-Yvelines – are still growing. They have good facilities, including a new cathedral at Evry and Disneyland Paris leisure park just outside Marne-la-Vallée.

Some older towns – Meaux, Mantes, Melun and Rambouillet – have been picked out to be **link towns**. They are to be developed as links with the regions that are neighbours to the Ile-de-France.

These towns have new housing, industries and offices as well as improved transport links, for example an express rail network. Future plans for transport include:

* the Orbitale – a 170km light rail system which would directly link the outer suburbs
* the Icare – a 150km underground toll motorway reserved for cars and light vans linking the new towns, the outer suburbs and the two airports.

Urban development in the city of Paris

Over the past 30 years the east side of Paris has been left behind in terms of development. Until very recently it suffered from poverty and neglect. Since the 1980s there have been schemes to improve two of the eastern districts – Bercy and Tolbiac (photo **C**). Bercy now has an

B Cergy-Pontoise is a new town developed as part of the urban development plans in the Paris region

C The district of Tolbiac in Paris has been improved as part of urban development schemes in the city

Any day now Parisians could be in shock. All it will take is for an anticyclone to descend on the city, giving it a couple of nice days of sunshine and stillness, for traffic fumes to build up. Then – hey presto – at 5pm one afternoon the authorities will decree that half the city's cars will have to stay off the road the following day. Even numbered cars will be used on even-numbered days, odd-numbered vehicles the rest of the time. The plan for Paris would be triggered if pollution reached 'Level 2' and if weather forecasts showed a risk of it reaching 'Level 3' the following day. Since 1994 Paris has hit 'Level 2' twenty times and 'Level 3' twice. Such a plan is not new in Europe. Athens has had a similar scheme in force for several years. But Paris is not Athens; it has less sunshine to react with car fumes, far less industry clustered around, and has arguably the best metro in the world as well as an extensive suburban railway. Yet Paris is beginning to choke a bit. Some three million cars flow in and out of the city every day, tempted in by the policy of Jacques Chirac, during his 17 years as mayor, of building a minimum of 5000 new underground parking places every year. Cars now lurk underneath virtually all its squares and wider boulevards, including the Champs Elysées. Peugeot and Renault also make a higher share of diesel engines, which consume less fuel but spew out relatively more pollutants, than their competitors.

D An extract from the *Financial Times*, 24 March 1997

international wine and food centre (including restaurants, conference facilities, wine bars, delicatessans and a cookery school). Apartment blocks, hotels and the American Center of Paris has been moved here. Tolbiac is still being developed. It now has the new national library (the world's biggest library) and when it is finished there will also be office space for 60 000 people and apartment blocks for 20 000 people.

Transport is also to be improved. There is the Meteor, an automated light railway, linking the districts with the Métro, and the express rail network from the suburbs.

FACT FILE

Modern and traditional attractions

Bercy and Tolbiac now have some of the most important new buildings in Paris. These include the Palais Omnisports du Bercy, a huge building with arenas for indoor sports, ballet, theatre and concerts. In Tolbiac the design of the Bibliothèque de France (national library) is very controversial. The building has four 80m high towers with lots of windows. Some people think that these towers spoil the skyline and that books stored here could be damaged by the sun's heat and light.

Many historic buildings and monuments make Paris very attractive for both residents and tourists. The most famous include Notre Dame, the Eiffel Tower and the Arc de Triomphe.

The problem of improving the roads in the city has not yet been solved. In the 1980s a scheme was proposed for a network of underground toll motorways (similar to the Icare but serving the city centre). Cars could have only come up to the surface in certain places in the city centre. However, it was thought that the motorways would encourage more cars to come into the centre and so make the problem worse. It was turned down.

There are also particular areas with much to visit such as: around the Avenue des Champs-Elysées where wealthy homes, fine hotels and the most expensive fashion houses are found; the Latin Quarter has been the student centre since the Middle Ages and has many pavement cafés and small restaurants.

Montreuil, a small town in France

▶ What are the physical and human features of Montreuil?

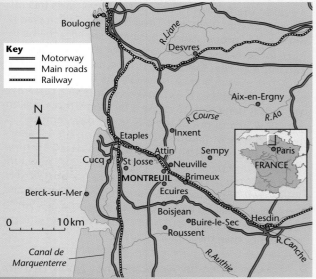

A Montreuil and surrounding area

History of Montreuil

Montreuil is just one of the many small towns in France. It is a walled medieval town in the Nord-Pas-de-Calais region. In medieval times it was a thriving port on the River Canche. Many goods were carried by barge to the quays in the town. Manufacturing industries developed to make use of these goods and mills were built to provide them with water power. However, by the end of the Middle Ages the river had begun to silt up.

Montreuil in the present day

2948 people live in the town, and many commute to work here. There are jobs in services such as tourist attractions, shops, offices, a hospital schools and a weekly market. There is also a range of light industries including the sale and distribution of agricultural machinery and the storage and distribution of agricultural products.

The land around Montreuil is excellent for arable farming. Wheat and sugar beet are most commonly grown.

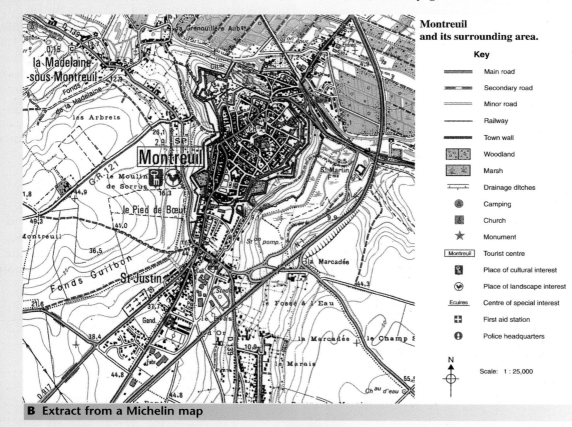

Montreuil
and its surrounding area.

Key

	Main road
	Secondary road
	Minor road
	Railway
	Town wall
	Woodland
	Marsh
	Drainage ditches
	Camping
	Church
	Monument
Montreuil	Tourist centre
	Place of cultural interest
	Place of landscape interest
Ecuires	Centre of special interest
	First aid station
	Police headquarters

Scale: 1 : 25,000

B Extract from a Michelin map

C Aerial photo of Montreuil

Two French tourists, aged 17 and 50, visiting Montreuil from Boulogne
We have come here for the day to visit the market and to walk around the town. It must be a nice place to live. There are no industries in the centre of the town, and there are interesting old buildings to see.

Young man and young woman living in Montreuil
We like living here but we wish the town was a bit livelier. There are some bars to go to, but there is nowhere for music or dancing. We often go to Boulogne with our friends in the evening or at weekends. There are not enough houses for younger people to live in. Most of the new houses that are being built are for the elderly. Younger people either live with their parents or move to other, bigger, towns.

A shopkeeper in Montreuil
I would like to build on to my shop to make it bigger, but I am not allowed to. This is because the town is a *monument historique*, and there are rules about what you can and can't do to the buildings here. The rules also mean that there can be very little new development in the town. Mind you, it means that the town looks attractive, and that brings in the tourists. This is good for business. Also, the market attracts people to the town to do their shopping.

Elderly couple who live in Montreuil
We are both very happy living here. I used to work for the Gendarmerie and my husband worked on the railways, so we both had jobs in the town. It is not so easy to find work here now because there are not many industries or offices in the town. Most people own a car, so they drive to other places to work. We do not want Montreuil to change. We have everything we need here.

D What people think of Montreuil

FACT FILE

A survey of visitors to Montreuil

Where do you live?			
Distance			
0–0/99km	**1–2km**	**3–8km**	**9–16km**
Montreuil (10)	Neuville (2)	Attin (3)	Buire-le-Sec
Ecuires (2)	Boisjean	Saint Josse (2)	Aranglo
	Brimeaux	Sempy	Berck-sur-Mer (3)
		Inxent	Haisnes
		Roussent	Abbéville
		Etaples	Aix-en-Ergny
		Cucq	Desvres
			Boulogne
			Hesdin
			Rouen
			London (3)
			Porthmadog (Wales)

			17+km
			Arras

Total number interviewed: 42 (Males: 21   Females: 21)

How did you get here?				
Type of transport:				
On foot	Bicycle	Bus	Train	Car
9	1	6	0	15

Car ferry	Mobile shop	Other	
4	6	1 (motorbike)	

Why have you come here?			
To shop	For work	Visit market	Visit family
6	10	5	1

Leisure	Attend school	Other
10	5	5

The information was collected over a weekend in Place du Général de Gaulle.

Manufacturing and services

▶ **How is manufacturing industry in France changing?**
▶ **How is the service sector changing?**

France's economic wealth is created by different types of production: primary (farming and mining), secondary (mainly manufacturing industries) and tertiary (services and high-tech industries). Each sector provides different amounts of wealth and different numbers and types of jobs – this is called the employment structure. Until recently, manufacturing industries provided much of France's wealth and jobs, but this has now changed.

	1970	1980	1990	1997
Primary	13.3	8.4	5.6	4.5
Secondary	37.9	34.8	28.9	25.3
Tertiary	48.8	56.8	65.5	70.2

A Changes in employment structure (%)

Decline in manufacturing

Since the second **oil crisis** in 1979, manufacturing industries have been in serious decline. For example:

- 100 000 jobs were lost in the iron and steel industry in the Lorraine and Nord regions.
- The textile industry went from 125 000 to 25 000 workers in the Nord region.
- Shipbuilding has just survived in Saint-Nazaire and Le Havre but was forced to close down in Dunkirk and La Seyne.
- The car industry has lost workers in Nord-Pas-de-Calais, Lorraine and Franche-Comté.

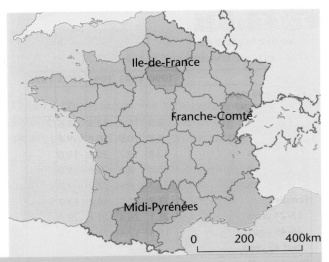

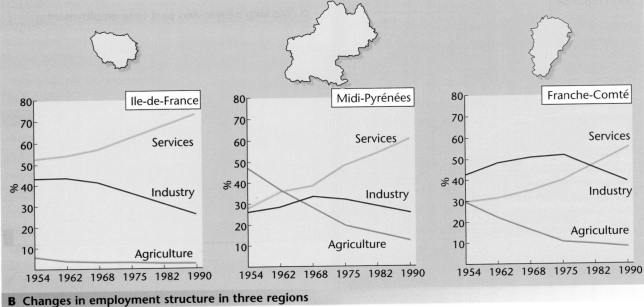

B Changes in employment structure in three regions

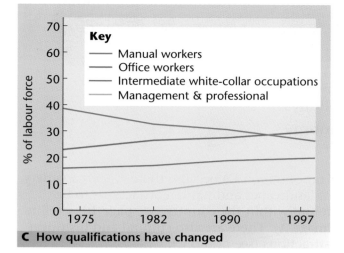

C How qualifications have changed

Growth of science parks

The industries that are gaining jobs are those referred to as 'high-tech', including information technologies, micro-electronics, robots and automation, space research and biotechnology. They often locate together in 'science parks' (also known as **technopoles** – see pages 46–47 and 52–53) on the edge of cities and near to universities. The largest science park is Paris-Sud. Other specialized technopoles are found in Toulouse (aerospace), Montpellier (biotechnology), Rennes (communications technology) and Grenoble (electronics).

Other services

New jobs have been gained in the tertiary sector, in consultancy, market research and advertising. Tourism has become very important, making money for the country and providing many jobs (see pages 36–37).

Effects of the changes

The new high-tech industries and services tend to locate in different regions from those that were important for manufacturing (figure **B**). This means that some regions are left with high unemployment.

Also, people who have been employed in older manufacturing industries do not generally have the skills needed for working in the new industries (graph **C**). Often they are unable to get new jobs because of this.

FACT FILE

The car industry in France

Distribution of car industry

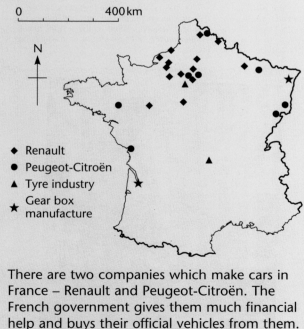

- ◆ Renault
- ● Peugeot-Citroën
- ▲ Tyre industry
- ★ Gear box manufacture

There are two companies which make cars in France – Renault and Peugeot-Citroën. The French government gives them much financial help and buys their official vehicles from them. Both companies are in the top five French companies by turnover. Between them they employ about 280 000 people and produce about 3 million cars a year. Both companies have factories in other countries: Renault in Portugal, Spain, Belgium and Slovenia; and Peugeot-Citroën in the UK. The car companies buy most of the parts they need from other national companies e.g. Michelin Tyres based in Clermont-Ferrand.

Car production

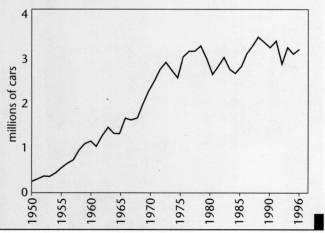

Tourism

▶ **Where do the French go for their holidays?**
▶ **Why is tourism important to the economy?**

People in France have more money to spend in their leisure time (table **E**). As a result, the demand for leisure facilities has grown and more holidays are being taken (graph **D**). French people take many of their holidays in France (graph **D**) because there is such a variety of landscapes and natural attractions to be found within the country (see page 10, satellite image **A**). There are also cultural and historical attractions (see photo **C**).

CASE STUDY: TOURISM IN RHÔNE-ALPES

Tourism has developed in the region of Rhône-Alpes mainly because of the mountains which make up about half of the area. Some of the world's best ski-slopes can be found here.

There are parts of Rhône-Alpes which either offer distinctive natural features (photo **B**) or cultural attractions in the large settlements like Lyons, and buildings of historical interest (photo **C**).

A An extract from the *Financial Times*, 23 February 1995

Foreign visitors redress balance

By Andrew Jack

Rhône-Alpes has an unusual challenge when it comes to tourism. It is not so much that it has too few visitors, but rather that it has too many. In the east of the region are the Alps, providing a range of mountain sports in both summer and winter, dominated by skiing. To the west are the wine valleys with worldwide reputation: the Loire, Rhône and Beaujolais.

To the south is the Ardèche, containing a network of prehistoric cave settlements and paintings including the latest discovery at Combe d'Arc, one of the most important,

dating from 20 000 years ago. All around are scattered chateaux and settlements, larger cities such as Lyons, Grenoble and St Etienne with their museums and old buildings, and small, hidden villages such as the hill-top cobbled streets of Perouges.

The seasonal variations in the number of visitors to the region present particular challenges for employees in the region, many of whom take part in annual migrations between ski resorts in winter and beaches in summer.

More worryingly, there is a danger of overcrowding. While skiers may complain of crowded slopes in the Alps during the winter and spring, perhaps the most troubling threat is to the fragile ecology of the Ardèche during the summer.

The main culprit is the French practice of the *grandes vacances*: the summer holidays in July and August, linked to the school break. Three-quarters of those visiting in mid-July are French.

B Ardèche gorge

C Old buildings in St Etienne

About 60 million tourists also come to France every year from other countries. Tourism is very important for the economy because it creates jobs, and tourists spend money while on holiday (table **F**).

	1970	1980	1990	1997
Gross disposable income (per head, in French francs)	11 081	37 056	77 781	93 802

E How much disposable income people have

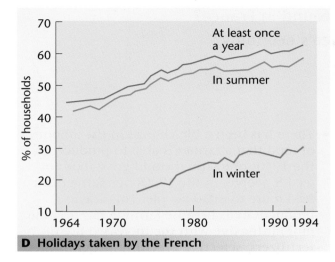

D Holidays taken by the French

i) Foreign tourist arrivals, 1996 (thousands)	
Belgium and Luxembourg	7 375
Canada	560
Denmark	821
Germany	13 378
Italy	5 299
Japan	578
Netherlands	4 415
Portugal	644
Spain	2 759
Switzerland	3 737
UK and Ireland	9 926
USA	2 603

ii) Money spent by foreign tourists in France
(French francs, billions)

1970	1980	1990	1996
7.3	34.8	109.9	145.1

F Spending by foreign tourists

FACT FILE

Leisure activities

As well as more money to spend on leisure activities people now have more time for them. This has resulted in a number of changes in the use of leisure facilities, some of which are shown in this table.

Changes related to leisure activities		
	1973	1993
books published	23 013	38 616
number of cinemas	4250	4402
visitors to national museums	7.4 million	16 million
ave. time watching TV	2hrs 42mins	3hrs 39mins

Young people and leisure

According to a survey in 1989, those under 25 spent 11.7 per cent of their money on leisure activities compared to an average of 6.5 per cent for older people. A survey carried out in 1995 reveals a lot of detail about what the money is being used for.

It was found that 12–14 year olds take part:
- in school and school-related activities e.g. trips to the theatre, museums and art galleries,
- outings suggested or organized by the family
- more individual activities e.g. video games.

Going to the cinema was common to both boys (91 per cent) and girls (89 per cent). Girls and young women of all ages were interested in the arts, e.g. dance and music, whilst boys and young men mentioned video games and sport as their interests.

French boys and girls have similar preferences for sport to children elsewhere in Europe:
- boys preferred football, with basket-ball second in popularity, for those between 14–16
- girls liked swimming best, followed by skating, dancing, gymnastics and basket-ball. Almost 20 per cent went riding and another 20 per cent played volley-ball.

Farming in France

▶ What different types of farming are found in France?
▶ What part does farming play in France's economy?
▶ How is farming in France changing?

The importance of farming

In the past, farming was very important to France because so many people worked on the land. This has now changed but farming is still important for different reasons:

- France is able to produce much more food than it needs and so is able to sell it to other countries. In fact France is the second largest food exporter in the world.
- Farming is the only way to earn a living in some of the rural areas of France. If people could not farm in these areas they would become unemployed. This would be bad for them as individuals and bad for the communities that they live in.

Changes in farming

Over the past 40 years farming has changed a lot (figure **C**).

- There has been a big change in the amount of food that a farmer is able to produce. In the 1940s one farmer could grow food to feed 5 people. In the 1990s one farmer can feed more than 30 people. This rise in productivity is because farming has become more **intensive** with the increased use of **fertilizers**, **selective breeding programmes**, **irrigation**. It is also because some farms have got bigger with larger fields so that machinery can be used more easily.
- Many farmers have given up farming and moved to towns for work. During the 1990s around 30 000 people left the land every year. Those who left tended to be the younger ones (figure **B**). Most of them left areas of France where the land is difficult to farm, usually because of the climate, relief and **accessibility**.

A A typical farm in Midi-Pyrénées

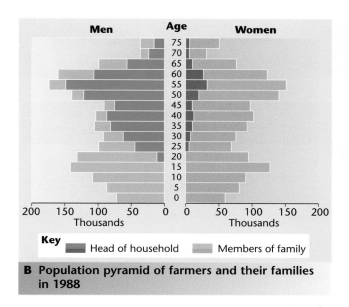

B Population pyramid of farmers and their families in 1988

Key: Head of household / Members of family

	1950	1990
% employed	27	6
Total employed (millions)	5.1	1.9
Average farm size (ha)	14	36
No. of farm holdings	2.3 million	900 000
Total area under farmland (million ha)	34.5	31.3
Drained land (million ha)	590	2083
Irrigated land (million ha)	539	1147

C Changes in farming, 1950–90

Farmers in these areas are not able to make a living very easily. Farms that remain in these areas tend to be small and **non-intensive** (photo **A**). Environmentalists argue that this type of farm is better for the environment because it is sustainable.

The Common Agricultural Policy

The Common Agricultural Policy (CAP) was set up as part of the European Community (now the European Union). Its aims were to:
• increase the amount of food produced
• make sure farmers had a fair standard of living
• make sure prices for food were reasonable
• keep prices and the supply of food at a steady level.

CAP has been successful in some ways but it has also caused problems such as the 'milk lakes' and 'butter mountains' in the 1980s. Guaranteed prices gave farmers **subsidies** for their crops and livestock – but the farmers with the largest farms benefited.

In 1992 CAP was reformed to cut down on the money spent on subsidies. This reform favours the most efficient farms whilst many of the poorest farmers suffer, although they need help the most.

FACT FILE

Fishing

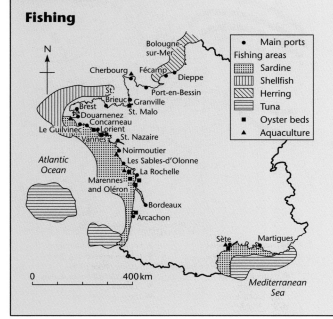

Fishing has always been an important economic activity in the coastal regions of France. As well as the main ports shown on the map there are small fishing boats operating from most coastal villages. The French eat a lot of fish – about 30 kilos per head in 1990, compared to 20 in the UK.

French fishing boats work all round the coast of Europe and north into the Arctic waters. The French fishing fleet is also able to use the fishing grounds around the eastern coast of Canada because two small islands there (Saint-Pierre and Miquelon) have remained French territory. They also fish off the western coast of Africa because of the links which have been kept between France and its former colonies like Senegal and Congo.

Energy

What energy resources does France have?

Sources of energy

As an industrialized country, France uses a lot of energy. The energy comes from different sources. The use of each source has changed over time because of economic and political factors (table **A**). One important factor is whether a source is domestic (French) or is imported.

	1991	1992	1993	1994	1995
Coal	7.4	6.8	6.2	5.4	5.5
Oil	3.4	3.4	3.3	3.5	3.1
Natural gas	2.9	2.8	2.9	2.9	2.7
HEP	13.8	16.2	15.2	18.0	17.0
Nuclear	73.5	75.1	81.7	79.8	83.7

A National energy statistics (million tonnes of oil equivalent).

B Coal and nuclear energy production

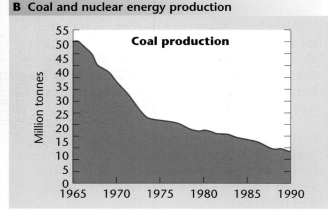

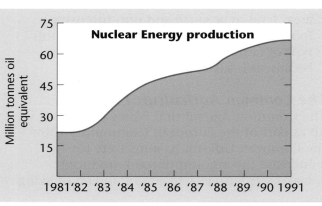

COAL

Coal was a very important source of energy in France until recently (figure **B**). In 1958 the total amount produced was 60 million tonnes (the highest amount ever). This was about 60 per cent of the energy being used in France, employing 300 000 miners. By 1989 only 13 million tonnes were produced by about 28 000 miners. Today some coal is imported.

The last mine on one of the main coalfields, Nord-Pas-de-Calais, was closed in 1991. Coal was always difficult and expensive to mine here because of thin, crooked seams. Also, the type of coal was bad for human health and many miners suffered from lung disease. However, 6500 miners still worked there in 1989. The environment in this area has been badly affected by spoil tips, derelict mine buildings and pollution of water and air.

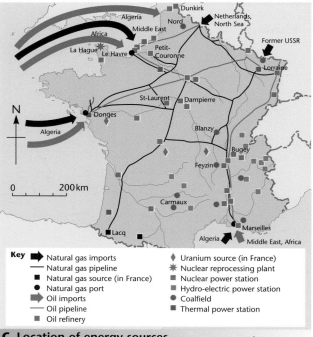

Key
- ➡ Natural gas imports
- — Natural gas pipeline
- ■ Natural gas source (in France)
- ● Natural gas port
- ➡ Oil imports
- — Oil pipeline
- ■ Oil refinery
- ◆ Uranium source (in France)
- ✳ Nuclear reprocessing plant
- ■ Nuclear power station
- ■ Hydro-electric power station
- ● Coalfield
- ■ Thermal power station

C Location of energy sources

NUCLEAR POWER

Nuclear power is now the main source for France's energy (figure **B**). In 1974 the French government began to invest in nuclear power stations. It takes seven years to build a reactor, so it was not until the early 1980s that nuclear power could be used. Recently some people have started to worry more about whether nuclear reactors are safe. Also, there are problems about dealing with nuclear waste which are similar to those in Britain – no one wants it in their backyard. A big advantage is that nuclear power is considered 'domestic' even though some uranium is imported. The amount needed is very small and the cost is relatively low. Nuclear power stations tend to be located near a water source, used for cooling, rather than close to the source of uranium (figure **C**).

HYDRO-ELECTRIC POWER

Hydro-electric power (HEP) has been developed in the mountains (see page 10) where many of the fast-flowing rivers are dammed. A tidal power station has also been built at Rance in Normandy. Both of these types of water power are renewable, non-polluting and domestic. However, only small amounts of electricity can be produced from each plant and they do affect the look of the landscape (figure **D**).

GAS AND OIL

Gas and oil are important sources. Both are used to generate electricity and so power stations are located near the ports (figure **C**). Like coal, they are fossil fuels and have many of the same disadvantages, such as being non-renewable and being sources of pollution. Also, most of the gas and oil used in France is imported, mainly from Russia, the Netherlands and Algeria. Since the **oil crises** in the 1970s, France has cut back on its use of oil.

D HEP plants are non-polluting but they do have a visual impact

FACT FILE

Mining
As well as coal, other natural resources are mined in France (shown in the table). Nowadays these do not play a big part in either the national or local economy. However, in the past some were more important, for example bauxite – the raw material for aluminium – was given its name after being discovered in 1821 near the village of Les Baux in Provence.

	Thousand tonnes	
Natural resource	**1970**	**1995**
aluminium	469	586
bauxite	2992	131
copper	34	186
iron	19 575	12 876
iron ore	18	0.5
nickel	11	10.4
silver	150	2.9
uranium	1476	950
zinc	258	310

Rhône-Alpes – a wealthy region

▶ Why is the Rhône-Alpes region considered wealthy?
▶ How does the region's economy affect people's lives?

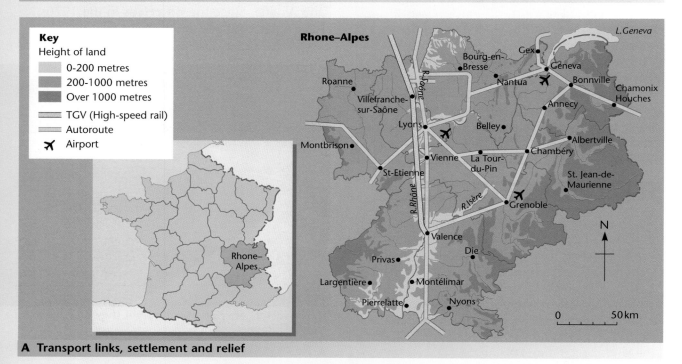

A Transport links, settlement and relief

Rhône-Alpes is France's second largest region. It makes up 8 per cent of the land and is home to 10 per cent of the population.

Corridor of communications

Rhône-Alpes is at the centre of networks of motorways, high-speed railways and air routes (map **A**). One of the reasons that industry has developed here is that Rhône-Alpes is an important corridor of communication between northern and southern Europe. A great deal of traffic, both passengers and freight, moves through Rhône-Alpes. This is likely to increase in the future and may cause problems of congestion.

The economy

Rhône-Alpes is second to the Ile-de-France for economic activity, with a high GDP, although their employment structures are different (figure **B** and **B** on page 34). Tourism is very important (see pages 36–37). Agriculture is less important mainly because of the region's relief.

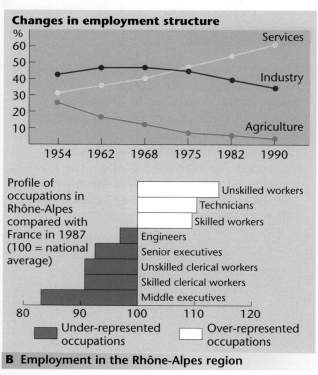

B Employment in the Rhône-Alpes region

C The chemical industry is particularly well developed in Rhône-Alpes

D Developing technopoles attract new high-tech industries

Rhône-Alpes is France's leading producer of many manufactured goods. Industries located here include oil refining, chemicals (e.g. Rhône-Poulenc in Roussillon and Saint-Fons – photo **C**), car production (e.g. Renault in Venissieux and Bourg-en-Bresse) and high-technology (e.g. Hewlett Packard in Grenoble). However, the distribution of industrial activity is very uneven. The east of the region has attracted more new industries than the west, with many of the region's **technopoles** located in and around Grenoble (photo **D**).

There are many national and international centres in the region, e.g. the Grenoble Nuclear Research Centre, the World Health Organization's International Cancer Research Centre. Much of the energy needed is produced by hydro-electric and nuclear power stations in the region.

Urban areas

Rhône-Alpes has more built-up areas than other regions of France (apart from the Paris region). There are three large cities: Lyons (second in size to Paris), Grenoble and Saint-Etienne. Lyons is becoming a prosperous and dynamic city. Saint-Etienne, on the other hand, still suffers from the loss of jobs in traditional industries. It has fewer jobs in the service sector than the other cities. Other settlements are also suffering from the closure of traditional heavy industries.

FACT FILE

The fire goes out of a smelting village
By David Owen

Mr Jean-Noel Guglielmi, deputy mayor of Riouperoux in the Rhône Alpes, looks at the overgrown rock face rising almost sheer behind the Pechiney aluminium factory 30 miles south-east of Grenoble. "There used to be no plant life over there," says Mr Guglielmi, "and no birds. In 10 years, that's really changed. But people used to say if there was smoke in the valley there was work in the valley."

Soon the wildlife may have more cause to celebrate. Cost cuts by Pechiney, Europe's biggest aluminium maker, means the Riouperoux plant's output of smoke and metal is to end.

In the grand scheme of things this little factory, with its four 25-tonne furnaces and its modest output of special alloys for the car industry, will scarcely be missed. But its closure, with the loss of 72 jobs, could make all the difference in the world to Riouperoux, a care-worn, smoke-blackened village of 1,400 people which has suffered years of slow decline. Its population has halved in 40 years. derelict buildings abound. The prospects of attracting another industrial employer do not look bright.

Yet Riouperoux appears to have some resources it could better exploit. For one thing, the Route des Alpes, bisecting the village, is regularly thronged with day trippers and tourists heading for the nearby mountains. Mr Marcel Blanchard, a union representative at the factory, says caustically that all the village gains from this is traffic jams. Nonetheless, Riouperoux, in its beautiful if rugged valley, looks better placed to cash in on tourism than many other hard-up rural communities.

Selling bread in the village's tiny bakery, Mr Jean-Paul Baudin has already cottoned on to the potential. "The factory is not what keeps us busiest," he says. "It's the tourists."

Furthermore, the village is within easy commuting distance of a large and reasonably vibrant city: Grenoble. It seems well positioned to attract more than its fair share of yuppies with a taste for rural life and a desire to be within easy range of both the pistes and the city office blocks. "Riouperoux won't be a dead village, but it will be a dormitory village," says Mr Bernard Grivel-Delillaz, a former paper plant worker serving pastis behind the bar of the Taillefer restaurant. "The village will still exist, but from an industrial point of view there will be nothing left."

Financial Times, 23 November 1996

Regional differences in France

▶ **What are the differences between France's regions?**
▶ **How have these differences changed?**

Measuring the wealth of regions

A country's wealth is measured in GDP (page 32). Table **A** shows the GDP made within the French regions divided by the number of people. This tells us how much wealth, on average, each person in a region makes.

Regional differences in the past

Over the last 30 years the regional differences in France have changed. Back in the 1950s and 1960s, the regions in the west and south of France were called 'the desert'. This was because there were hardly any industries there. Most industries were found around Paris and in the north-east, but today many of these have declined. At the same time new industries and services have set up in the west and south (map **B** and figure **D**).

France = 100	
Ile-de-France	152.9
Haute-Normandie	103.8
Alsace	103.7
Rhône-Alpes	99.1
Champagne-Ardenne	92.6
Centre	91.7
Aquitaine	90.7
Provence-Alpes-Côte d'Azur	90.7
Franche-Comté	90.0
Bourgogne	88.5
Picardie	85.8
Pays de la Loire	85.4
Midi-Pyrénées	83.1
Basse-Normandie	82.3
Lorraine	82.0
Auvergne	81.4
Poitou-Charentes	81.3
Bretagne (Brittany)	80.2
Nord-Pas-de-Calais	80.0
Langedoc-Roussillon	77.9
Limousin	77.2
Corse (Corsica)	74.1

A GDP per head in the regions

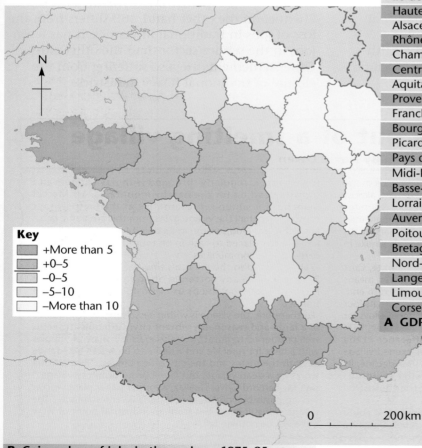

Key
- +More than 5
- +0–5
- –0–5
- –5–10
- –More than 10

0   200 km

B Gain or loss of jobs in the regions, 1975–85

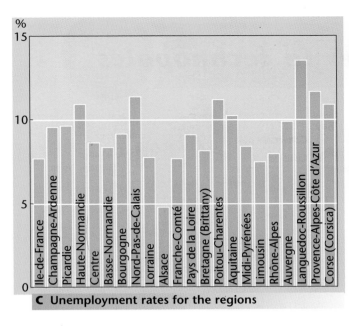

D Tourism has brought new life to some regions

C Unemployment rates for the regions

Regional differences today

Today, regional differences still exist but the pattern is different:

1 The Paris region in the Ile-de-France: still very wealthy even though some industries have moved away as part of the **decentralization policy**.

2 The regions of Rhône-Alpes, Alsace and Provence-Alpes-Côte d'Azur: generally wealthy regions with many new industries.

3 The regions of the west and south, from Lower Normandy to Languedoc-Roussillon: these have become richer as new industries have moved in and tourism has grown.

4 The declining industrial regions of the north and east including Nord-Pas-de-Calais, Lorraine, Normandy, Franche-Comté and Burgundy: traditional industries, like coal-mining and ship-building, have declined. They have not been replaced by new high-tech industries (figure C).

5 The rural deserts found along a **transect** from the Ardennes to the Pyrénéés (see map **A** on page 48), including Corsica. Farming has declined. No new industries have arrived.

These five divisions give a general picture. There are also inequalities within regions – for example, Nice is rich whilst Marseilles has many social and economic problems – and between rich city centres and poor suburbs.

FACT FILE

Employment and income

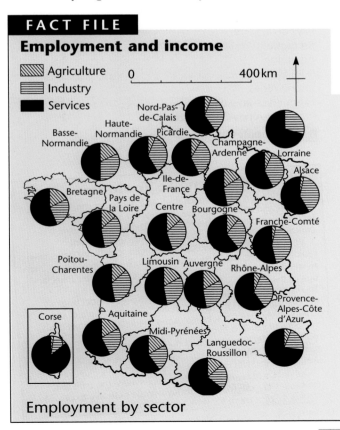

Employment by sector

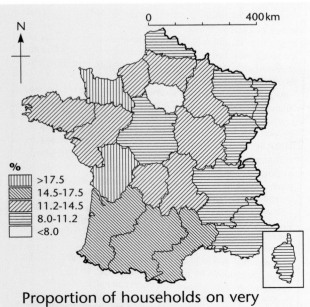

Proportion of households on very low incomes by region

%
>17.5
14.5-17.5
11.2-14.5
8.0-11.2
<8.0

From conversion poles to technopoles

▶ **What policies has the government used to tackle regional differences?**

▶ **What part do technopoles play in helping poorer regions?**

Government policy and conversion poles

Since the 1950s, government policies have encouraged new industries and services to locate in regions with high unemployment. In 1984, places with the most serious economic problems were chosen as **conversion poles** (map **A**). The government helped new industries set up here with money to:

- retrain workers
- improve housing and roads
- reclaim old industrial land
- modernize old industries.

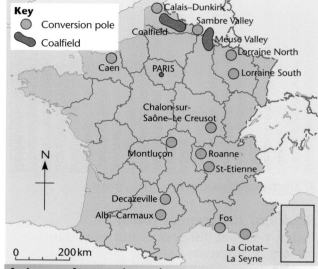

A A map of conversion poles

Region	No. of technopoles
Ile-de-France	3
Centre	1
Basse Normandy	1
Nord-Pas-de-Calais	1
Lorraine	2
Alsace	2
Pays de la Loire	2
Bretagne	3
Aquitaine	1
Midi-Pyrénées	3
Rhone-Alpes	7
Languedoc-Roussillon	2
Provence-Alpes-Côte d'Azur	2

B Technopoles in France

C About Toulouse

Little farms and little industry

By John Ridding

Beyond the high-tech centre of Toulouse and the industrial towns of Tarbes, Albi and Rodez lies a vast rural region – bigger than Belgium or the Netherlands. A world apart from the space research and electronics design conducted in the regional capital, it has its own economic structure and its own concerns.

At the root of the region's various problems lie weaknesses in its agricultural centre. Despite steady growth in recent years, farms in the Midi-Pyrénées are relatively small – 51 per cent are less than 20ha, and only 13 per cent bigger than 50ha. More seriously, the region lacks agricultural industry.

To counter these challenges, the region's agricultural organizations have focused on increasing the value of production. One example is the seeds industry, which has seen considerable development in production and research. Large companies, such as Rustica and France-Mais, have set up in the region. Successes include resistant and high-yield seeds for maize, which have seen strong demand from French farmers.

Traditional products are also being steered towards a higher value, for example by introducing labelling, and establishing brand image. From Roquefort cheese to garlic, cassoulet and beef, local producers are seeking to establish brand identities.

An extract from the *Financial Times*, 18 May 1994

Welcome to Toulouse

Toulouse has built a reputation as a dynamic, modern city. Aviation and space industries, electronics, information technology and biotechnologies are the key sectors that have contributed to our city's solid economic development.

With a population of 700000, France's fourth city has grown rapidly over the last thirty years to become Europe's Space and Aviation capital, France's first university campus after Paris, and one of the country's leading research centres.

Toulouse's development has been controlled, respecting the city's all important quality of life. With its jumble of old streets, lively café terraces, colourful markets and russet roofs, this ancient city has become home to a unique mix of high-tech industry and the arts, of Renaissance heritage and youthful ambition. It is a city on a human scale, easy to stroll about in, with masses to do and see.

Our aim is to make Toulouse a place where the skills and techniques of yesterday and today mingle naturally to provide an ideal environment for new talent to build the future.

Dominique Baudis Deputy–Mayor

Decentralization policy and technopoles

The government restricted industries setting up in the overcrowded Paris region. This is called the policy of **decentralization**. Many new high-tech and research industries moved to the south and west, where some then set up in **science parks**, called **technopoles**. Many technopoles have developed because of the decentralization policy but some, like those in the Ile-de-France, are the result of free market forces.

Technopoles – some examples

- Technopoles were set up in the Midi-Pyrénées in 1983 and 1988. Aerospace and space research industries have located in Toulouse (photo **D**) and Labège. These include the European Airbus project and research centres for Air France.
- In Brittany (Bretagne), technopoles are located in Brest, Quimper and Rennes. They were set up between 1984 and 1988. Rennes has many telecommunication industries, including Telecom France.
- Languedoc-Roussillon has technopoles in Montpellier and Nîmes. They were set up in 1982. Montpellier specializes in **biomedicine**, **pharmaceuticals** and **agribusiness**.

Benefits of technopoles

Technopoles have many benefits for the region and for France. The industries that locate in

D Toulouse

them are in great demand in national, European and global economies, providing goods and services which are vital in the business world today. They generally make good profits and so can pay high rates, taxes and rents for land and buildings. Salaries are also high because employees need to be highly qualified.

The government policies of decentralization and of encouraging technopoles have helped some of the less developed regions to attract industries. These regions have experienced general increases in employment and wealth. However, not everyone in the regions has benefited from the new industries, either because they live in rural areas (figure **C**) or because they lack the skills needed by the new industries.

FACT FILE

Contrasts in the region of Midi-Pyrénées

Looking at the figures and statistics for the whole of the region of Midi-Pyrénées gives the impression of rapid economic development and success. However there are great contrasts within the region. The **conurbation** of Toulouse has grown very quickly both in terms of population and economy. It is a very large urban area, where about one-third of the region's population lives, with a thriving and modern economy, dominated by modern industries including electronics and high–tech companies. This contrasts strongly with the rest of the region which is generally very rural, dependent on agriculture and has a sparse, ageing population. The other towns of any size, such as Tarbes and Montauban, are 10 times smaller than Toulouse and their few traditional industries, such as textiles and furniture, are declining.

Main enterprises in Midi-Pyrénées		
Name	**Employees**	**Activity**
Aérospatiale	8500	Aeronautics
Groupement des industries d'armement terrestre	3800	Arms
Cablauto SGE	2800	Car equipment
Motorola semi-conducteurs SA	1800	Electrical equipment
Pierre Fabre Médicaments	1700	Pharmaceuticals
Société d'économie mixte de transport de l'agglomération mération toulousaine	1500	Urban transport
Tissus Roudière	1400	Textiles
GEC Alsthom SA	1300	Electrical equipment
Siemens automotive SA	1300	Car manufacturing
Thomson CSF	1200	Electronics

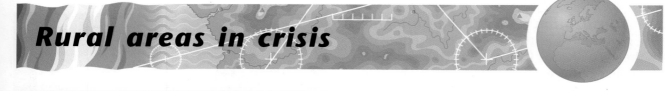

Rural areas in crisis

▶ **Where are the poorest rural areas in France?**
▶ **What problems do they suffer from?**
▶ **What could be done to tackle the problems?**

The poorest rural areas and the problems they face

A recent study by the government shows that about 40 per cent of France is made up of rural areas which are very poor. They have very bad economic and social problems. Some of the worst-affected areas are located in the 'empty diagonal' (map **A**). Along the 'empty diagonal' most areas have:

- fewer than 17 people per km²
- 13.4 per cent of the population aged over 75
- lost 12 per cent of their population between 1975 and 1990
- 30 per cent of the work-force in farming.
- income from farming which is about 40 per cent of what an average French person earns
- a poor quality of life – this is measured by looking at how many people have cars and whether there are services nearby, e.g. schools, doctors.

The problems get worse

These problems of the poorest rural areas are likely to get worse. People are still moving away, particularly the young. As no one is moving in, farmland is abandoned and the land then gets overgrown with scrub. Land abandoned like this has led to forest fires becoming a problem in some areas (photo **B**).

The solutions?

The problems of these poor rural areas often get publicity. Some organizations are trying to preserve rural life by solving the problems. They organize demonstrations and run campaigns. One campaign had the slogan 'Sheep are cheaper than a Canadair' (the type of plane that carries water to drop on forest fires).

Government money is being used in two main ways:
1 Farmers are given subsidies by the government so that they can continue to farm their land.
2 Farmers are given grants to convert farm buildings into holiday homes (called *gîtes* – figure **C**) or craft workshops. They will then be able to earn money from these as well as from farming.

Another way has been tried by one mayor of a rural area. He advertised for large families to move from the cities into villages in his region. As a result, one family of ten moved from Roubaix in the industrial north to La Porcherie in Limousin.

THE 'EMPTY DIAGONAL'

N

0   200 km

Key
Urban areas
Worst-affected areas suffering from economic and social problems

A The poorest rural areas of France

B Forest fires can occur when land is abandoned

Rescorles

Converted stone barn
Sleeps 2 adults, 3 children

Nearest Town/Shops: Plescop (2 miles), Vannes (4 miles), sea (17 miles)

Accommodation: 3 bedrooms (1 double; 1 twin; 1 single), kitchen, living room, shower room, 2 wc's, garden

"Comfortable stone cottage, Ideally placed for exploring coast"

Rescorles was renovated by the owners in 1992 and is a house of immense character. It is ideally situated to explore the coastline, the Golfe du Morbihan and the hilly interior of Southern Brittany. The living room has exposed stone walls and is comfortably furnished including some antique furniture. The fitted kitchen is smart and modern with tiled surfaces, built-in hob and oven. The 3rd bedroom in the converted attic has a wooden ceiling and velux window. Outside is a lovely terrace, driveway and large garden with swings and climbing frames. Rescorles offers the opportunity of staying in a rural cottage of a high standard in a tranquil setting. Plescop has a choice of local shops, whilst the large hypermarkets on the outskirts of Vannes should be used for major shopping expeditions. Vannes is a beautiful old town dominated by a fortified chateau overlooking the port. The nearest beaches are at St.Philibert or Sarzeau.

C An advertisement for a gîte

FACT FILE

Profile of a rural region: the Auvergne

The Auvergne is in the Massif Central and is crossed by the 'empty diagonal'. Clermont-Ferrand, the regional capital (see page 25), is the only city in the region. The region is mountainous with one main valley – that of the river Allier – in the north. The population density is just half of the national average and the population is unevenly distributed, with most people living in the Allier valley. Many young people are leaving the region to look for work in modern industries and services. Tourism provides some jobs in the service sector. Tourists are attracted by the mountain scenery and volcanic landscapes.

	M + F 1000	M + F %	M %	F %
< 15	221.1	16.7	17.6	15.9
15-24	192.4	14.6	15.2	13.9
25-39	279.8	21.2	22.1	20.3
40-54	238.5	18.0	18.8	17.4
55-64	155.6	11.8	11.6	11.9
≥ 65	234.3	17.7	14.7	20.6
Total	1321.7	100.0	100.0	100.0

Population by age

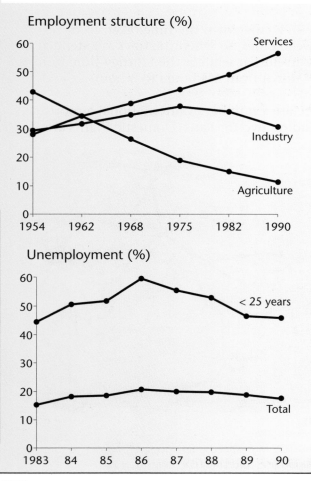

Employment structure (%)

Services

Industry

Agriculture

1954 1962 1968 1975 1982 1990

Unemployment (%)

< 25 years

Total

1983 84 85 86 87 88 89 90

The importance of transport

▶ Why does France need good transport links?
▶ What problems are associated with improving transport links?

Road, rail and air transport

France has a large motorway (*autoroute*) network (map **A**). Some *autoroutes* have tolls, which means that drivers have to pay to use them. Certain routes, for example Paris to Marseilles, are particularly busy.

In the 1980s, France developed a high-speed train system called the *Train à Grande Vitesse (TGV)*. It needs purpose-built track and engines that can reach speeds of 270–300km per hour. The first line was opened between Paris and Lyons. There are plans to extend the track over the next 20 years (map **A** and extract **D**).

The *TGV* cuts down the time taken to travel between cities, so when the track is extended to Marseilles it will cut the journey-time from Paris down from 4.5 hours to 3 hours.

There are a number of international airports, including two for Paris. Domestic flights are also important because of the size of the country. Airports for some of the cities furthest away from Paris are particularly busy because of this, for example Nice has over 6 million passengers a year.

Transport issues

Good transport is needed so that products, raw materials and people can be moved from place to place quickly and cheaply. Efficient transport links are vital to poorer regions that are trying to develop industries and services. The extension of motorways and the high-speed railway to these regions is an important part of regional development plans.

The most wealthy region of France, the Ile-de-France which includes Paris, is at the centre of motorway and high-speed train networks. Some people have criticized the *TGV* for mainly bene-fiting the Paris region. Other criticisms are about the impact of new transport routes on the environment (figure **D**). Overcoming environmental problems can be very costly (photo **B**).

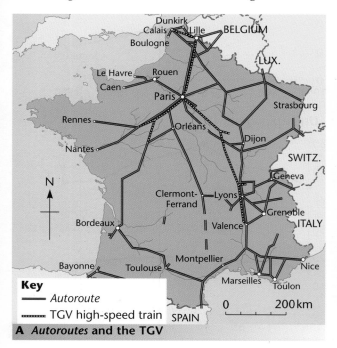

Key
— *Autoroute*
····· TGV high-speed train

A *Autoroutes* and the TGV

B Building roads like this – along the coast of Provence-Alpes - Cotes d'Azur – takes considerable time and money

CASE STUDY: SOUTHERN FRANCE

If southern France is to be economically successful it will need better transport links which will include connections with Spain and Italy (see page 55 on the economic development of this area). There are already plans to develop the transport networks with:
- a *TGV* tunnel between Perpignan and Figueras, Spain, by 2005 and
- a road tunnel between Nice and Turin.

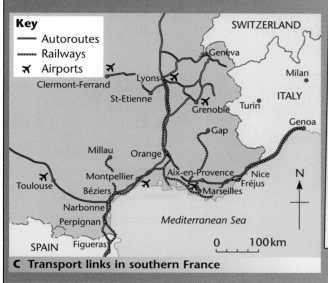

Key
— Autoroutes
···· Railways
✈ Airports

C Transport links in southern France

Bold plans run into opposition
By George Graham

A drive along the A8 motorway linking Aix-en-Provence to Nice and the Italian frontier demonstrates some of the problems involved in laying out the infrastructure of southern France. A series of curves and gradients as the A8 cuts its way through the mountainous countryside of Provence points out the difficulty of building high-speed road or rail links in this terrain.

As plans are drawn up for the next century, however, the engineering problems of building high-speed roads and railways have to be faced, for southern France's traditional ground transport axes – down the Rhône valley and through a more or less narrow corridor along the coast – are approaching saturation. By road, the plan is to expand the north–south routes by complementing the main Paris–Lyons–Marseilles motorway with new routes to the east – from Grenoble via Gap to Marseilles – and to the west – from Clermont-Ferrand to Montpellier.

By rail, planners aim to extend the TGV high-speed train south from Lyons to Marseilles, cutting the Paris–Marseilles journey-time by 11/2 hours to 3 hours. In theory, at least, the TGV tracks will branch east to Fréjus, cutting Paris–Nice to 4 hours and allowing an extension to Italy, and west to Montpellier and Barcelona.

This TGV plan, however, has run into fierce local opposition. While Marseilles politicians and business people are desperately keen for the TGV to come to their city, the inland districts through which the railway must pass have risen in fury against what they see as a Parisian scheme that will devastate the Provençal countryside.

D An extract from the *Financial Times*, 25 March 1991

FACT FILE

The Channel Tunnel

The Channel Tunnel links England, between Folkestone and Dover, to France just west of Calais. It is about 30km in length and takes approximately 30 minutes to travel through. The train service which uses the Tunnel, Eurostar, runs from London to Paris. It is possible to travel on the train as a foot passenger, or to take your car in custom-built carriages. The trains also carry freight.

The areas of England and France which include the tunnel portals (entrances) have been affected by the construction of the Tunnel. The transport networks which lead to and from the Tunnel have been improved. There has been an increase in the economic development around it, with industries wanting to benefit from the easy access between the two countries. However, the Tunnel has been criticized. Some people feel that it was too expensive, and that it will lead to traffic congestion and too much industrial development. There have also been concerns about safety, particularly if there were to be another fire in the Tunnel (there was one in 1996).

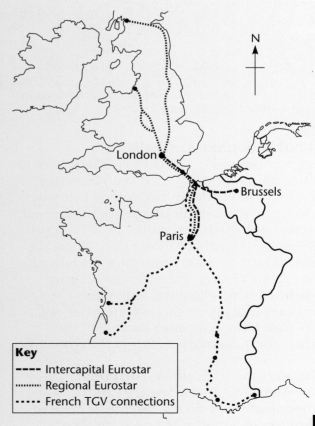

Key
---- Intercapital Eurostar
········· Regional Eurostar
····· French TGV connections

Sophia Antipolis Science Park

▶ What types of industry locate in a Science Park?
▶ What are the attractions of Sophia Antipolis?
▶ What effects does Sophia Antipolis have on the surrounding area?

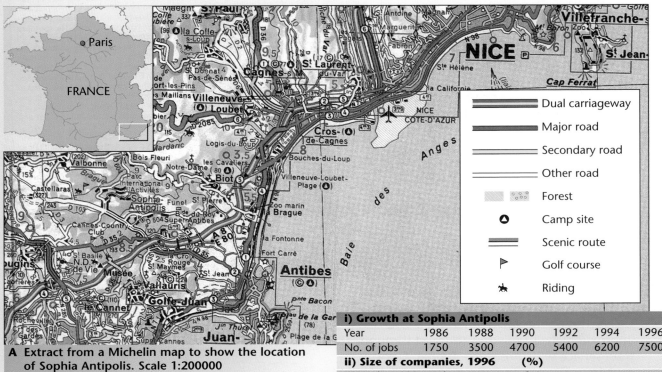

A Extract from a Michelin map to show the location of Sophia Antipolis. Scale 1:200000

Map legend:
- Dual carriageway
- Major road
- Secondary road
- Other road
- Forest
- Camp site
- Scenic route
- Golf course
- Riding

What is Sophia Antipolis?

Sophia Antipolis is a Science Park near Nice in southern France (Map A). It is an important centre for industries in electronics, computer science, telecommunications, health care and **biotechnology**. It was started in 1974 as part of France's decentralization policy. There are now more than 1000 companies, covering an area about 4553ha. The main activities are research and development, with some production of high-tech specialist goods, e.g. CD-ROMs. The companies here are in the tertiary or **quaternary sectors** of the economy.

Attractions of Sophia Antipolis

The companies in the Science Park are 'footloose'. They do not need to be close to resources or a market but need excellent

i) Growth at Sophia Antipolis

Year	1986	1988	1990	1992	1994	1996
No. of jobs	1750	3500	4700	5400	6200	7500

ii) Size of companies, 1996 (%)

	(%)
More than 100 employees	2.4
50–100 employees	3.2
10–49 employees	21.0
Less than 10	73.4

iii) Types of company, 1996 (%)

	(%)
Distribution	12
Education and research	6
Health services and technologies	6
Information sciences	23
Other services to companies	51

iv) Foreign companies, 1995

Country	No. of companies	No. of jobs
Germany	5	86
Spain	2	506
UK	8	369
Italy	7	248
Others (Europe)	22	412
North America	48	2055
Asia, Japan, Korea	2	49
Others	3	87
Total	**97**	**3812**

B About the companies at Sophia Antipolis

C Nice offers many attractions for those living and working at nearby Sophia Antipolis

D A great deal of planning has gone into the physical environment of Sophia Antipolis

communications and a highly-skilled work-force. Sophia Antipolis offers:

- Closeness to Nice airport, which has direct flights to 33 countries
- The best telecommunications equipment available, including fibre-optic cable networks
- Special training programmes provided by the University of Nice (map **A**)
- Nearby Nice and the French Riviera with attractions which appeal to prospective employers and employees (photo **C**)
- A pleasant environment, with two-thirds of the site set aside for green space and all buildings fitting in with strict codes so that they look good (photo **D**)
- Large areas for recreation and sports, e.g. tennis, art galleries, and restaurants.

Effects of Sophia Antipolis on the locality

Sophia Antipolis brings benefits to the area:

- The companies provide well-paid, interesting jobs for local people: 'Ten years ago I would have gone to Paris after high school. But because of Sophia Antipolis, I could stay here and go to the University of Nice and get a technical degree.' (Owner of an Internet services company)
- The University has expanded because it works in partnership with some companies at Sophia Antipolis.
- The companies of Sophia Antipolis have a **multiplier effect** on jobs: they attract other businesses and services into the area.

However, not everyone benefits:

- Skills and qualifications are needed to get well-paid jobs at Sophia Antipolis, and local people may not have these. Some companies bring their highest-paid employees with them, so only less well-paid jobs are left for local people.
- The development has caused increased traffic on roads to and from the site.

- House prices have increased as more people move into the area.
- The natural vegetation of the site, called **maquis** and **garrigue**, has been replaced with an artificial landscape.

FACT FILE

The region of Provence-Alpes-Côte d'Azur
The overall number of jobs in Provence-Alpes-Côte d'Azur (PACA) is growing faster than the national average. The Science Park at Sophia Antipolis provides a pole of economic activity and there is also an increasing number of jobs in the region related to tourism. However, the region's unemployment is still quite high. This is partly because the population has grown quickly due to the number of people moving to PACA. Also, the concentration of heavy industries at Fos-Etang de Berre, just outside Marseille, still provides many jobs but has declined in recent years. Employment opportunities are not evenly distributed, with 8 out of 10 jobs concentrated in the three coastal departements, particularly those in the east of the region.

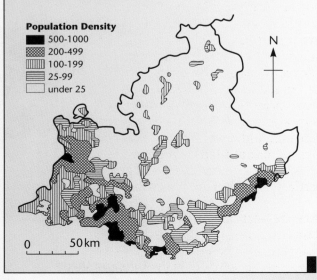

Population Density
- 500-1000
- 200-499
- 100-199
- 25-99
- under 25

N

0   50km

6 FRANCE AND THE WORLD

France and the 'hot banana'

▶ How will France affect and be affected by the changing economy of the EU?

Core and periphery

Like most individual countries, the European Union (EU) has areas that are wealthier than others (map **A**). In the past there was one main **core** area with most economic growth and poorer areas outside of this, in the **periphery**.

In the 1970's and 1980's the core was between London, Frankfurt and Milan, including Paris and Amsterdam on either side. It is still important today and is called the **'hot banana'** due its shape.

More recently the pattern has changed because:
• countries have joined the EU, and their wealthier areas provide other cores
• some industries have declined and others developed elsewhere.

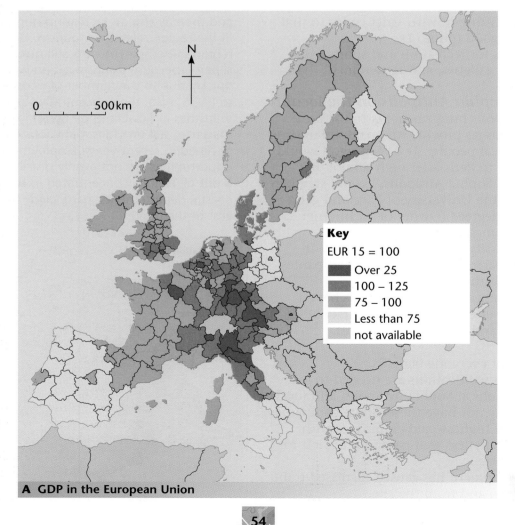

Key

EUR 15 = 100

■	Over 25
■	100 – 125
■	75 – 100
■	Less than 75
■	not available

A GDP in the European Union

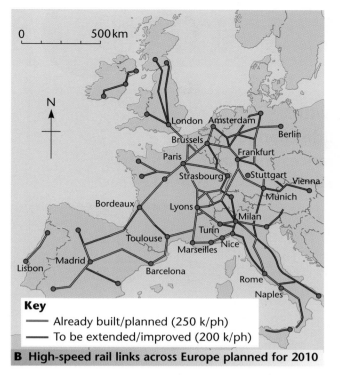

Key

— Already built/planned (250 k/ph)

— To be extended/improved (200 k/ph)

B High-speed rail links across Europe planned for 2010

The importance of transport

In the past the Pyrénées and the Alps were barriers to trade. Now, a 5km motorway tunnel is being built under the Pyrénées, and there are plans to tunnel through the Alps to shorten the road route between Nice and Turin. There are also ambitious plans to extend the high-speed railways (map **B**). (See pages 50–51 for more details on transport developments.)

Benefits and problems

Some French regions will benefit from being in an 'economic corridor'. Parts of southern France are poorer and less industrialized than the regions of Italy and Spain on either side of them. The French hope that the Spanish and Italians will invest in them as well as in their own regions. Once industries and services are established in an area they have a **multiplier effect** by attracting other businesses.

There are problems too:

- Local people may not benefit from new companies moving in, e.g. Montpellier has attracted new companies but many have brought their highly-paid employees with them, so only the lower-paid jobs are offered locally.
- Even within an 'economic corridor' there may be areas that miss out on economic growth, e.g. Marseilles may be left out as the motorway cuts inland about 100km north of the city.
- Economic development can bring problems of traffic congestion and environmental damage.
- Areas in the periphery cannot compete with the concentration of economic growth in the core and in 'economic corridors', and so need government and EU grants to help attract economic development.

'Economic corridors'

Companies in different cores do much business with each other and so '**economic corridors**' develop between them – areas within 'corridors' benefit from the movement of goods and people along them.

After Spain joined the EU, three 'economic corridors' developed between:

- Barcelona and Stuttgart
- Barcelona and Toulouse
- Barcelona, Nice and Turin – planners call this one the '**Mediterranean arc**'.

FACT FILE

Japanese industries in European countries.

Date	UK	France	Germany	Spain	Italy
1983	15	10	20	18	7
1985	32	30	34	22	8
1987	53	33	45	29	11
1989	68	38	53	33	15
1990	91	83	64	41	24
1992	181	119	101	64	39
1993	195	128	111	67	47

Foreign investment in France

Of the European Union countries investing in France, the Netherlands invests the most, followed by the UK. The USA is the biggest foreign investor in France.

Japan started to invest in Europe during the 1980s. By making products in the European Union (EU) Japan can avoid some of the regulations on imports which were introduced at that time. If a product is made in the EU it can be moved free of tax anywhere within the Union.

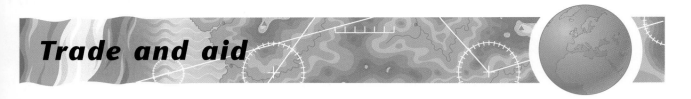

Trade and aid

▶ Which countries does France trade with?
▶ How and why has the pattern of trade changed?
▶ Which countries receive aid from France, and why?

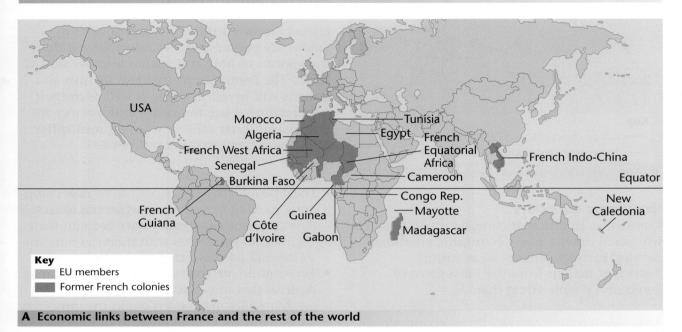

A Economic links between France and the rest of the world

Imports and exports

France has economic links with many other countries (map A). These links include trade, aid and investment. Trade with other countries involves **imports** and **exports** (figure B).

The **balance of trade** of a country is the difference between the value of imports and the value of exports. This may vary from year to year (graph D).

Trade with the EU and former colonies

There are rules for trading within the EU which mean that taxes cannot be put on goods that are imported from other EU countries. In the past, countries used to do this in order to make the price of all imported items higher than the price of the same items made within the country.

1 = French francs 2 = %	Exports		Imports	
	1	2	1	2
Agriculture, forestry and fishing:				
basic	78.6	5.3	54.2	3.8
processed	139.5	9.4	106.7	7.6
Energy	36.7	2.5	113.5	8.1
Metal goods	122.5	8.2	119.4	8.5
Chemicals	223.9	15.0	221.9	15.7
Investment goods	407.7	27.4	352.7	25.0
Passenger cars and other transport equipment	196.7	13.2	166.1	11.8
Non-durable consumer goods	227.8	15.3	227.2	16.1
Miscellaneous	54.6	3.7	48.2	3.4
Total	**1488.0**		**1409.9**	

B Goods imported and exported, 1994

Exports to:	% of total	Imports from:	% of total
Germany	15.9	Germany	16.6
UK	10.1	Italy	9.8
Italy	9.3	USA	8.8
Belgium/Lux.	8.1	UK	8.3
Spain	8.0	Belgium/Lux.	8.0
USA	6.5	Spain	6.7
Netherlands	4.7	Netherlands	5.0
Other trading partners	37.4	Other trading partners	36.8

C Main trading partners, 1997

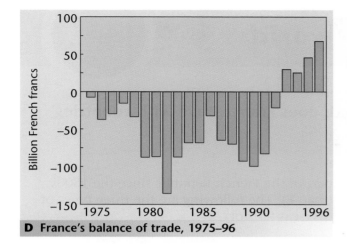

D France's balance of trade, 1975–96

% of total French Overseas Development Aid															
6.3	5.1	4.8	4.5	3.4	3.4	2.9	2.4	2.1	1.9	1.6	1.3	1.3	1.2	1.1
Côte d'Ivoire	French Polynesia	New Caledonia	Egypt	Cameroon	Morocco	Senegal	Algeria	Congo, Rep.	Gabon	Madagascar	Burkina Faso	Mayotte	Tunisia	Guinea

F Major recipients of French foreign aid, 1995/96

France, like the UK, used to have a large colonial empire. Today these former colonies are independent countries but there are still economic links between them and France, although this is changing (figure E).

But although taxes are still placed on imports from outside the EU, the terms of trade with the former colonies are usually more favourable than those with other countries.

Foreign aid

The colonial past influences which countries receive **foreign aid** from France (F).

France gives a lot of aid compared with other EU countries (see page 62). Aid is useful to some French companies as well as to the receiving countries. Sometimes aid comes with the condition that any work to be done, e.g. building roads, has to be done by French companies

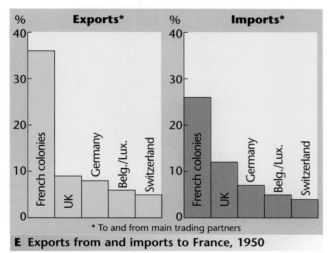

E Exports from and imports to France, 1950
* To and from main trading partners

FACT FILE

Trade with other countries

Imports are the items that France buys from other countries. These include raw materials for French manufacturing industries, and manufactured products and services that are needed either because France does not make or provide them itself, or to give a wider choice for people to buy. Exports are items that France sells to other countries. France is the largest food producer and exporter in Western Europe.

European trade with North Africa, 1990

Country	Belgium/Lux.		France		Germany (West)		Spain		UK	
	Exports	Imports	Exports	Imports	Exports	Imports	Exports	Imports	Exports	Imports
Morocco	18.2	19.0	157.9	163.0	43.1	50.4	35.5	54.4	15.7	17.5
Algeria	42.3	20.6	150.5	260.0	73.7	85.0	65.5	43.0	36.2	–
Tunisia	21.2	20.5	128.3	73.0	56.0	41.9	–	–	–	–

▶ **What links, other than trade and aid, does France have with countries outside of the European Union?**

French 'ownership' of land overseas

France has a number of overseas *départements* (departments) and territories which have been part of the French Republic since the 1800s (map **E**). The following are the three types of overseas territory.

GUADELOUPE: AN EXAMPLE OF AN OVERSEAS DÉPARTEMENT

Guadeloupe is made up of eight inhabited islands in the Caribbean (map **A**). About 40 per cent of the population lives around Pointe-à-Pitre, the main industrial and commercial centre. Sugar-cane is grown in the rest of Grand-Terre, with some tourism and market gardening in the east. Basse-Terre has banana plantations, and sugar-cane is cultivated in Marie-Galante. The *département's* balance of trade is poor, partly because there is virtually no manufacturing. Two-thirds of Guadeloupe's trade is with France. Until recently many of the islands' young adults moved to France to find jobs, although this pattern changed in the 1980s. This movement has affected the population structure (table **D**).

Tourism has become one of the *département's* main economic activities. There are many natural attractions (photo **C**) for tourists, including forests, mountain ranges and beaches. However, there is stiff competition from other Caribbean countries.

A The islands of Guadeloupe

Population	Thousands, 1990	People/km², 1990	% change, 1980-90
	385	227	17.7
Unemployment		**(1990) %**	
		31.1	
Employment	**% agriculture**	**% industry**	**% services**
	11	18	72
GDP/person, 1986		**(EUR = 100)**	
		38	

B Guadeloupe: statistics

C The traditional image of a tropical island is one of Guadeloupe's attractions for tourists

Age	Total (thousands)	% M + F	% M	% F
Less than 15	96.3	24.9	25.7	24.0
15–24	78.0	20.2	20.7	20.0
25–39	95.1	24.6	24.7	24.2
40–54	57.8	14.9	14.7	15.1
55–64	26.7	6.9	6.6	7.2
More than 65	33.0	8.5	7.6	9.5
Total	**386.9**	**100.0**	**100.0**	**100.0**

D Population structure, Guadeloupe, 1990

- **French overseas *départements*** There are four – Guadeloupe, French Guiana, Martinique and Réunion. Each is governed by a Prefect who is appointed by the French Government, and they have their own Courts of Appeal. They have the status of regions, like, for example, the Ile-de-France region. This means they have a Regional Council, elected locally with responsibility for some economic, social and cultural issues. Overseas *départements* send representatives to the French National Assembly and the Senate in Paris, and to the European Parliament in Strasbourg.

E French overseas *départements* and territories

- **French overseas territories** These are French Polynesia, the French Southern and Antarctic Territories, New Caledonia, and the Wallis and Futuna Islands. They are governed by a High Commissioner, who is appointed by the French Government. Each territory also has locally – elected representatives who sit in the French National Assembly and the Senate.

- **French overseas *Collectivités Territoriales*** Mayotte and St-Pierre and Miquelon are administered by a Prefect who is appointed by the French Government. The Prefect is helped by a locally elected General Council. The Council is represented in the French National Assembly, the Senate and the European Parliament.

FACT FILE

Present day links between France and Vietnam

Foreign capital investment in Vietnam

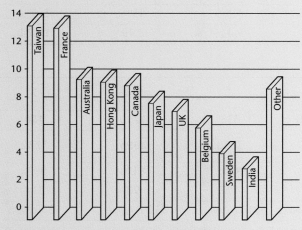

Vietnam became independent from France in 1954. For many years the communist government of Vietnam was opposed to contact with any western capitalist country, but recently there has been a change in policy. As a result of this change, links between Vietnam and France have started to be rebuilt. Much business is now done with France, for example Vietnam Airlines has replaced Russian-made aircraft with jets from Airbus Industrie of Toulouse, and the training of airline staff is done with the help of Air France. Another example is that half the medicines and pharmaceutical products sold in Vietnam are made in France.

Number of visitors to Vietnam and their countries of origin

	1992	1993	1994	1995
Taiwan	70,143	95,077	184,241	224,004
France	19,204	47,683	96,669	119,202
Japan	19,119	29,638	65,055	117,763
USA	14,563	23,361	42,438	54,368
UK	6,662	17,276	36,863	51,817
Hong Kong	13,985	15,224	23,186	21,093
China	1,738	8,352	14,326	19,407
Others	202,171	198,330	252,274	315,908
Overseas Vietnamese	80,858	152,672	202,046	260,294
Total	**440,000**	**669,862**	**1,018,062**	**1,358,182**

Statistics

	UK	CHINA	FRANCE	SOUTH AFRICA	USA
Total area (km²)	244 880	9 596 960	551 500	1 221 040	9 809 431
Total population (millions)	58.3	1210.0	58.8	44.0	263.6
Population density: people per km²	243	130	107	35	28

Population

	UK	CHINA	FRANCE	SOUTH AFRICA	USA
Birth rate (per 1000) people	13	17	13	27	15
Death rate (per 1000) people	11	7	9	12	9
Life expectancy (male and female)	74M 79F	69M 72F	75M 83F	54M 58F	73M 79F
Fertility (children per female)	2	2	2	4	2
Population structure: 0–14 15–59 60+	19% 61% 21%	27% 65% 9%	20% 61% 19%	37% 57% 6%	21% 62% 17%
Urban population	90%	29%	74%	57%	77%

Environment and economy

	UK	CHINA	FRANCE	SOUTH AFRICA	USA
Rate of urban growth per year	0.3%	4.3%	0.4%	3.0%	1.3%
Land use (%): arable grass forest	27 46 10	10 43 14	33 20 27	10 67 4	19 25 30
% workforce in: farming industry services	2 28 70	73 14 13	6 29 65	13 25 62	3 25 72
GNP per person (US$)	$18 700	$620	$24 990	$3160	$26 980
Unemployment	8.3%	2.8%	11.6%	45%	5.6%
Energy used (tonnes/person/year)	5.40	0.35	5.43	2.49	10.74

Society and quality of life

	UK	CHINA	FRANCE	SOUTH AFRICA	USA
Infant mortality (deaths per 1000 births)	6	38	6	5.4	7
People per doctor	300	1000	333	1750	420
Food supply (calories per person per day)	3317	2727	3633	2695	3732
Adult literacy	99%	70%	99%	81%	99%
TVs per 1000 people	434	31	407	98	814
Aid received or given per person	$53 given	$3 received	$137 given	$10 received	$33 given
Spending on education (as % of GNP)	5.3	2.4	6.0	3.8	7.0
Spending on military (as % of GNP)	4.0	3.7	3.4	3.0	5.3
United Nations Human Development Index (out of 1.0)	0.92	0.59	0.93	0.71	0.94

Figures are for 1992–97. Source: *Philip's Geographical Digest* (United Nations, World Bank). The Human Development Index is worked out by the UN. It is a summary of national income, life expectancy, adult literacy and education. It is a measure of human progress. In 1992, the HDI ranged from 0.21 to 0.94.

General

Longest river: River Loire (1012km)
Highest mountain: Mont Blanc (4807m)
Currency: franc and centimes
Capital: Paris

Religion: Catholic (about 80%)
Local government units: 22 regions, 96 departements
Types of cheeses: over 400

Social

Student population in 1992 (in thousands)

	Number of Students	% enrolling in higher education
United Kingdom	1178	21.2%
France	1584	36.4%
Spain	1169	36.6%
Germany	1720	28.7%
Italy	1373	28.3%
European Union (12 countries)	8299	24.4%

Some changes between 1973 and 1993

	1973	1993
Number of households	17.6 million	22 million
Annual increase in purchasing power	4.4%	2.2%
Rate of inflation	8.5%	2%
Number of part-time jobs	787 000	2.27 million
Working population	22.3 million (1975)	24.6 million (1991)
Annual number of divorces	39 000	106 000
Checking accounts	29.33 million	60.65 million
Income tax as % of household budget	6.12%	8.92%
Housing units without basic conveniences	46%	8.6% (1990)
Number of megastores	245	976
Number of passenger cars	14 million	24 million
Superhighway network	2040km	7109km
Rail network	35 145km	32 730km
Number of telephone lines	5 million	30 million
Households with a washing machine	14.9%	93.7% (1991)
Books published	23 013	38 616
Cinema theatres	4250	4402
Visitors to national museums	7.4 million	16 million
Stereo owners	8%	61% (1991)
Daily newspaper readers	55%	41%
Average daily time watching television	2hrs 42mins	3hrs 39mins

Economic

Main crops, wine, meat and dairy products

	Output (m tonnes)	World ranking	EU ranking
Cereals			
Wheat	35.9	3	1
Maize	14.4	5	1
Barley	9.5	5	3
Sugarbeet	30.7	1	1
Potatoes	6.5	10	4
Wine	**5.9**	**2**	**2**
Meat			
Beef and veal	1.7	7	1
Pork	2.2	4	2
Dairy			
Milk	25.7	5	2
Cheese	1.7	2	1
Butter	0.5	4	2

Foreign aid donated (in millions of US Dollars)

	Total ODA 1990	Total ODA 1994	1994 ODA as a % of GDP
Australia	955	1087	0.38%
France	6874	8447	0.64%
Japan	9054	13 238	0.29%
Norway	1205	1137	1.05%
Sweden	1998	1703	0.90%
United Kingdom	2630	3085	0.30%
United States	10 194	9851	0.15%

Leisure (billions of francs spent)

Radio and television	17
Hi-Fi and video recorders	17
Printing and publishing	27
Press	36
Sound and video recordings	21
Art and antiques	11
Cinema	5
Performances and other services	30
Source: Ministry of Culture	

Household consumption (1993, in %)

	France	Germany	United Kingdom	Italy	Spain	Sweden	Japan	United States	Switzerland
Food and tobacco	19.1	16.8	21.6	20.7	21.8	22.0	20.8	13.1	27.6
Clothing	6.5	7.4	6.2	10.1	8.9	7.2	6.0	6.6	4.4
Housing, heat and light	18.9	18.2	18.5	14.8	12.6	25.7	18.6	19.3	19.3
Furniture and household equipment	7.8	8.4	6.7	9.5	6.6	6.4	6.5	5.6	5.2
Medical and health services	9.3	14.2	1.4	6.6	3.8	2.6	10.5	15.3	10.1
Transport and communications	16.7	15.9	17.9	12.2	15.4	18.1	11.0	14.5	11.9
Leisure, education and culture	7.6	9.2	9.7	9.2	6.5	9.7	10.4	10.0	10.4
Other goods and services	14.1	9.9	18.0	16.9	24.4	8.3	16.2	15.6	11.1

Glossary

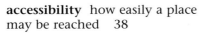

accessibility how easily a place may be reached   38

agribusiness farming and processing of food often carried out by transnational companies   47

avalanche a rapid fall of mud, rock, snow, or ice down a slope   13

balance of trade the difference between the value of goods exported and the value of goods imported   56

biomedicine medical study of environmental stresses on humans, especially during space travel   47

biotechnology technology based on biology rather than physics, e.g. genetic engineering   52

birth rate the number of births in a year per 1000 of total population   18

boulevard a wide, straight avenue   26

continental type climate a type of climate found near the centre of large landmasses: temperatures are extreme in winter and summer, and precipitation is low   12

conversion pole a place within an economically depressed area chosen by the government to be a growth pole, i.e. a centre for new economic growth   46

core a favoured and successful area in which jobs, people and services become concentrated   54

death rate the number of deaths in a year per 1000 total population   18

decentralization policy a government economic policy that encourages the outward movement of people, jobs and services away from the core areas   44, 46

deltas natural features built up where a river deposits its load at its mouth or in other places where its flow is suddenly slowed down   16

demographic transition a simplified way of describing how the changes in birth and death rates over time affect the total number of people in a country   18

dependency ratio the ratio between people in work and those who are not   19

drought a period of several months without rain   12

'economic corridor' area lying between two core areas which benefits from the movement of goods and people between them   54

exports goods and services sold by one country to others   56

fertility rate the number of children born to each woman   19

fertilizer material used to fertilize soil; it can be organic (manure) or artificial (chemicals)   38

'footloose' type of industry that does not have to locate near resources or a market   52

foreign aid money, technical expertise or food that is given by wealthy countries to poorer countries to help them deal with their problems. It can also benefit the donor countries, e.g. contracts for their companies to undertake projects like road-building   7

garrigue a type of scrubland in very dry areas   53

gross domestic product (GDP) the wealth created in a country   32

gross national product (GNP) a measure of the wealth created by a country's businesses both at home and abroad   32

'hot banana' name given (because of its shape) to one of the core areas within the European Union   54

immigrants people who come into one country from another   20

imports goods and services bought by one country from others   56

indented used to describe a coastline that is uneven, with bays and headlands   4

intensive farming getting maximum output by using high inputs of machinery, irrigation and other technologies   14, 38

interior inland area of a country, away from coasts   4

irrigation watering the land by artificial means such as sprinklers, channels, etc.   38

landmass huge area of land   12

link towns a number of old established towns, located away from Paris conurbation and on the edge of the region of the Ile de France, which have been chosen by planners to be encouraged to develop. They are used as links between the Ile de France and the neighbouring regions   28

maquis a type of scrubland in dry areas   53

Mediterranean 'arc' the 'economic corridor' running through southern France along the edge of the Mediterranean Sea, which links the core areas of northern Spain and northern Italy   54

Mediterranean type climate type of climate with hot, dry summers and mild winters named after the climate of the area around and including the Mediterranean Sea   12

migration movement of people from one place to another   18

mistral a cold wind that blows south down the Rhône valley   13

multiplier effect how economic growth and success in an area can attract and encourage more growth and development   52, 54

natural increase the growth in population as a result of the number of births being greater than the number of deaths   18

natural population changes changes in population totals resulting from the difference between death and birth rates   22

net migration the balance between the numbers of people moving into an area and those moving out   22

new towns settlements created as part of urban development plans; people are encouraged to move to them from large cities that are suffering from problems of overcrowding   28

non-intensive farming farming that uses human labour and natural procedures so generally producing less than if chemicals and sophisticated machinery are used   38

oil crises times in 1973 and 1979 when the oil-producing countries put up the price of oil which caused problems for those countries that depended upon its use   40

periphery an area that falls below the level of economic development and standards of living found in the core area   54

pharmaceuticals industry that makes or markets medicinal products   47

population density the number of people living in a specific area   22

population distribution the pattern of where people live   22

precipitation moisture in the atmosphere which falls to the ground as rain, hail, snow or sleet   12

prevailing wind the wind which blows from a particular direction (e.g. the west) most often   13

quaternary sector part of the economy that includes high-tech industries involving new technologies   52

range of temperature the difference between the highest and lowest temperatures experienced in a specific area   12

rural areas countryside areas   24

science park an industrial development with high-tech industries, particularly those involved with research and development   46, 52

selective breeding programmes the breeding of animals which, by carefully choosing the type of animal to breed from, will change the animals in some way to make them more useful for agribusiness   38

subsidies money paid, usually by governments, to help keep a business or farm running   39

transect a line taken across an area along which a survey or sampling is carried out   44

technopoles name given to science parks in France   46

urban areas towns and cities   24

urban development plan devised by the government (either local or national) to deal with urban problems such as overcrowding and traffic congestion   28

Finding out more about France

France maps
http://www.lib.utexas.edu/Libs/PCL/Map_collection/france.html

France tourism & travel – general information
http://www.fgtousa.org/GENINFO.htm

France travel & tourism – regions of France
http://www.fgtousa.org/regionalin.htm

FranceWay Rhône-Alpes
http://www.franceway.com/regions/rhonealp/index.html

General information and statistics
http://www.insee.fr

Maps of Europe
http://www.lib.utexas.edu/Libs/PCL/Map_collection/europe.html

Meteo France (temperature, climate)
http://www.meteo.fr/

Paris Tourism Information
http://www.paris.org

Sophia Antipolis Science Park
http://www.saem–sophia–antipolis.fr

Toulouse townhall
http://www.mairie–toulouse.fr

Welcome to FranceWay tourism and travel
http://www.franceway.com/welcome.html

Yahoo! France websites
http://dir.yahoo.com/Regional/Countries/France/

Index